OCR & EDEXCEL

Crime and Punishment

Investigations

WILLIAM PARKER
HISTORY DEPT

COLIN SHEPHARD
ROSEMARY REES

Exaltation of FARO's Daughters.

Hodder Murray

A MEMBER OF THE HODDER HEADLINE GROUP

Mark schemes

Mark schemes for the Source Investigations in Part 2 can be downloaded free of charge from www.hoddersamplepages.co.uk. Alternatively, you can call 020 7873 6000 and ask for the Educational Marketing department.

Orders: please contact Bookpoint Ltd, 130 Milton Park, Abingdon, Oxon OX14 4SB. Telephone: +44 (0)1235 827720. Fax: +44 (0)1235 400454. Lines are open from 9.00 to 6.00, Monday to Saturday, with a 24-hour message answering service. You can also visit our websites www.hoddereducation.co.uk and www.hoddersamplepages.co.uk

© Colin Shephard and Rosemary Rees 2005

First published in 2005
by Hodder Murray, a member of the Hodder Headline Group
338 Euston Road
London NW1 3BH

All rights reserved. Apart from any use permitted under UK copyright laws, no part of this publication may be reproduced in any material form (including photocopying or storing in any medium by electronic means and whether or not transiently or incidentally to some other use of this publication) without the written permission of the Publisher, except in accordance with the provisions of the Copyright, Designs and Patents Act 1988 or under the terms of a licence issued by the Copyright Licensing Agency.

Layouts by Black Dog Design
Illustrations by Tony Jones/Art Construction, Phil Garner/Beehive
Typeset in 11/12 pt Bodoni Book by Fakenham Photosetting
Printed and bound in Dubai

A catalogue entry for this title is available from the British Library
ISBN 0 7195 7977 5

Contents

Acknowledgements

Photo credits

Cover & frontispiece National Portrait Gallery, London; **p.1** Werner Forman Archive; **p.3** British Museum P178; **p.4** British Museum P190; **p.5** British Museum BMC 16430; **p.6** *both* Museum of London; **p.7** Angelo Hornak/Corbis; **p.12** British Museum BMC 16430; **p.18** Handschriften und Inkunabel Sammlung, Benediktinerabtei Lambach (Cod. Cml LXXIII f.64v); **p.19** Mary Evans Picture Library; **p.20** Kobal Collection; **p.23** Corpus Christi College, Cambridge Parker Library; **p.24** National Library of Scotland, Edinburgh; **p.26** *both* Fotomas Index; **p.27** Fotomas Index; **p.29** Fotomas Index; **p.30** *both* Fotomas Index; **p.33** *t* Fotomas Index, *b* British Museum BMS 69; **p.36** *tl* from *Crime and Punishment: a study across time*, Roger Whiting (Stanley Thornes), *tr* from *Crime and Punishment in England and Wales*, Eldon Smith (Gower), *b* Ogen's Cigarette Cards, Robert Opie Collection; **p.37** *l* National Maritime Museum, *r* print by Thomas Rowlandson, British Museum BMC 11627; **p.38** National Library of Australia, Canberra/Bridgeman Art Library, London; **p.39** *t* Thomas Rowlandson, National Library of Australia, Canberra, *b* Mary Evans Picture Library; **p.41** 'Dogs at Eagle Hawk Neck' from *The Adventures of a Griffin*, London 1867, National Library of Australia, Canberra; **p.44** *both* from *Sweeney Todd*, Peter Haining (Boxtree); **p.45** Photostage/Donald Cooper, Felicity Palmer and Thomas Allen, Royal Opera, Covent Garden, December 2003; **p.48** British Museum BMS 13266, **p.50** British Museum BMS 5947; **p.51** British Museum BMS 14332; **p.52** *tl* British Museum BMC 16430, *bl* Illustrated London News Picture Library, *r* from *Crime and Punishment: a study across time Teacher's Book*, Roger Whiting (Stanley Thornes); **p.53** Punch Picture Library; **p.54** Illustrated London News Picture Library; **p.55** The National Library of Wales; **p.56** Punch Picture Library; **p.59** *t* Hulton Getty, *b* British Library Newspaper Library 121A; **p.62** Hulton Getty; **p.63** *l* photo Victor Console for London News Photo Agency Ltd/Public Record Office, *r* Hulton Getty; **p.66** *all* Imperial War Museum, London; **p.67** British Library Newspaper Library 803; **p.68** *t* Illustrated London News Picture Library, *b* British Library Newspaper Library LD 116; **p.71** *both* John Frost Historical Newspaper Services; **p.72** *both* Punch Cartoon Library; **p.73** Hulton Picture Library; **p.74** Fotomas Index; **p.75** *t* British Museum BMS 14187, *b* Hulton Deutsch; **p.76** *tl* British Museum, *bl*, *tr* & *br* Mary Evans Picture Library; **p.77** *l* Mary Evans Picture Library, *r* Museum of London.

t = top, *b* = bottom, *l* = left, *r* = right, *c* = centre

Written sources

p.18 A from *The English: A Social History 1066–1945*, reprinted by permission of HarperCollins Publishers Ltd. © Christopher Hibbert 1994; **p.24** K from *Crime and Punishment through Time* by Ian Dawson, 1999, John Murray; **p.28** J from *The English: A Social History 1066–1945*, reprinted by permission of HarperCollins Publishers Ltd. © Christopher Hibbert 1994; **p.34** I from *The Gunpowder Plot* by R Crampton, 1990; **p.35** A from *The English: A Social History 1066–1945*, reprinted by permission of HarperCollins Publishers Ltd. © Christopher Hibbert 1994, C Colin Shephard; **p.40** I from *The Fatal Shore* by Robert Hughes, 1987, The Harvill Press; **p.43** D from *Sweeney Todd* by Peter Haining, 1993, Boxtree; **p.63** E from *The Suffragette Movement* by Sylvia Pankhurst, 1931; **p.67** E quoted in *Britain and the Great War*, Greg Hetherington, 1993, John Murray; **p.71** E quoted in *The General Strike* by Margaret Morris, 1976, Penguin Books.

Every effort has been made to trace all copyright holders, but if any have been inadvertently overlooked the Publishers will be pleased to make the necessary arrangements at the first opportunity.

How to use historical sources

During your study of the history of crime and punishment you are going to be using lots of historical sources to find out about the past. You will also have to answer questions about sources in the examination. The first section of this book has been written to give you some help with answering these questions.

Why it's important to know something!

Some people think that source questions are easy because you do not need to know anything – you can work out the answer from the source. How wrong they are. It's true that you need to study the sources carefully, but to make sense of them you need to know quite a lot about the topic as well. To see how important knowledge is, study the source below. See if you can work out what is happening in the picture and what the message of the artist was. Make a list of as many points as you can.

● **SOURCE 1**

How many of the following points did you get?
- It shows a Japanese woman who has married a western man.
- The baby (shown with his nursemaid) is the product of their marriage.
- The baby is shown as violent and has a beard and lots of hair because the Japanese thought of all westerners as 'hairy barbarians'.

And what was the purpose of the picture?
The drawing is obviously anti-western. It is a warning to Japanese girls not to marry the horrible barbarians (westerners) by showing what will happen if they do – they will have a child who is hairy and aggressive! Of course, the artist does not really think that babies like this one would be born. He is using this threat to get across the idea that westerners are horrible and so the Japanese should have nothing to do with them.

How do we know all this?
The picture was drawn in the 1860s when westerners were beginning to make contact with Japan. Commodore Perry, an American, had made the first contact in 1853. He was followed by other westerners who wanted to trade with Japan. Some of the Japanese did not want anything to do with the westerners. They thought the westerners were uncivilised barbarians and wanted them to go away. The picture was clearly drawn by someone of these views.

You probably did not work all this out! After all, you are not studying the history of Japan. But you can probably now see that to understand what the picture is about you need to know something about the background.

Study the drawing on the page opposite. Its subject is something you should know about. With a partner, discuss what is happening in the drawing. Then look at the points below and see how many you came up with.

- You probably recognised this picture. You probably knew straight away that it is about a convicted criminal being taken to be executed at Tyburn, London. Tyburn (where Marble Arch is today) was famous for its gallows and was the main place of execution in London. The procession has just reached the gallows. It would have taken the procession about two hours to get from Newgate Prison to Tyburn. All along the route there would have been crowds of well-wishers. Women would have given the criminal bunches of flowers, men would have shaken his hand and wished him well.
- You will have seen that the picture was drawn in 1747. You will know this was the time of the Bloody Code when many offences, even minor ones like stealing a spoon, were punished by hanging.
- You will have known that the death penalty was used as a deterrent – to try to scare people into not committing crimes.
- You will have known that executions were carried out in public. People would go along to watch with their family as a day out. There was a fairground atmosphere. Often the person about to be executed would be a hero to the people and would make a speech before being hanged. There were eight hanging days at Tyburn every year. These days were called 'Hanging Fairs'.
- You probably know that executions at this time did not work as a deterrent. How could they when people did not regard them with horror but saw them as a form of entertainment? You probably also know that juries often found prisoners not guilty because they thought it was wrong to execute someone for a minor offence. This actually led to the number of hangings going down! There was a growing number of people at this time critical of the number of offences that carried the death penalty. They said it was not working. Is the artist of this drawing one of those critics?

What do you think was the message of the drawing? Was the artist in favour of public executions or against them? See if you came up with the points given below the drawing on the page opposite.

● **SOURCE 2**

Tom, being taken to Tyburn in a cart. With him are his coffin and a clergyman who is trying to get Tom to repent of his sins and save his soul!

The title tells us that Tom, the condemned man, was young (probably a teenager) and was guilty of a minor crime – he was just an apprentice and he is described as 'idle', which suggests he got into bad ways through being a bit lazy and not taking his work seriously.

A grandstand for spectators, so they could get a view of the hanging. You can see the framework of the gallows just in front of the grandstand and the hangman smoking his pipe calmly! Women often saw the victims as heart-throbs – you can see a woman in the grandstand throwing flowers to Tom. At the bottom of the picture there is a woman throwing oranges. Everyone was there to watch the prisoner die in a brave and noble way. However, there is also a man holding a dog by its tail. He is about to throw it – but who at? There are also men (probably drunk) fighting.

The IDLE 'PRENTICE Executed at Tyburn.

In the coach is the clergyman from Newgate Prison where Tom had been kept. This clergyman made a lot of money by selling accounts of the exploits of men about to be executed.

Tom's mother weeping with her head buried in her apron. She seems to be the only person not having a good time. Can you see the pickpockets under her cart? Elsewhere there are refreshment sellers.

At the bottom of the picture a ballad-seller is selling a ballad about Tom's 'last dying speech'. Note how the artist has drawn this figure and the prison clergyman (who are both making a profit from the execution) as the only ones who are looking directly at the viewer of the drawing. Everyone else is watching Tom. Why has the artist done this?

A print by William Hogarth, published in 1747.

What is the message of the drawing?

You need to answer this question by using the details in the drawing and what you know about what was happening at that time.

The artist has tried to make the scene look as horrible as possible.

- He has shown the fighting and pickpockets to make the point that executions do not deter criminals – they actually give them an opportunity to fight and steal from people.
- He has shown that the prisoner is a hero to many people. This reinforces the point that executions did not deter people from committing crime.

- The artist also thinks it is horrible and degrading for people like the clergyman and the ballad-seller to make money from executions. In fact, the overall message seems to be that public executions degrade everybody involved – the prisoner, the crowd, the clergymen and the street sellers.

Let's put all this together with the fact that in the eighteenth century the death penalty was used for hundreds of minor crimes, that it was not successful as a deterrent, and that there was a growing number of people criticising its use. It now becomes clear that the artist was one of these people who thought that the constant use of the death penalty, and the spectacle of public executions, was wrong.

Making sense of unusual sources

Because the history of crime and punishment is such an unusual topic, some of the sources are going to be rather unusual. This makes them all the more interesting. See if you can make sense of the two sources that follow.

● **SOURCE 3**

In the background are doctors who are ignoring what is going on. This is to show how dissections are beneath them and are carried out by inferiors like surgeons.

Surgeons invited pupils and friends to watch. Look at their faces. What are their reactions to the dissection?

The artist has a pulley and rope pulling the head up to make the corpse look alive. This is connected with people's fears of surgeons dissecting people who were still alive.

Are the surgeon and his assistants made to look cruel and callous or careful and sensitive by the type of knife held by the surgeon and by the fact that one of his assistants is gouging out the eye of the corpse?

Why has the artist drawn a noose around the corpse's neck?

Why has the artist drawn a dog eating the corpse's heart?

An engraving called 'The Reward of Cruelty', 1751.

This drawing shows the body of Tom Nero being dissected. In the eighteenth century a certain number of bodies of executed criminals were handed over to the Company of Surgeons every year for dissection, for the benefit of their students. Nero had begun his life of crime by being cruel to animals (this is the cruelty in the title of the picture). He later murdered his mistress and was hanged. His body was handed over to the Company of Surgeons for dissection. This was regarded as a fate worse than death. Christians believed that their bodies would be resurrected at the Day of Judgement. This could not happen if your body had been dissected. The fact surgeons carried out dissections made people scared of them and added to the view that they were cruel and not bothered about the suffering of their patients. There was also a fear that if the hangman did not do his job properly prisoners might be dissected while they were still alive. This happened in 1740 to William Duell who suddenly sat up during his dissection. Thankfully, the surgeons had not got very far. Duell was given some wine and was later reprieved from the death penalty.

Use the drawing and all the information above to see if you can answer this question, 'What message did the artist want to give to criminals about dissection?'

Cartoons

The drawings we have been looking at so far are cartoons. You can see that the artists deliberately did not draw realistic pictures. What they drew was often fantastic, exaggerated, even mad. They did this to get a message across.

Is this cartoon realistic – did policemen talk to water pumps? Of course not. Does this mean the cartoon has no use to us as historians? Of course it doesn't. What we have to do is work out what point the artist was making.

   Look at the cartoon carefully. In pairs discuss the questions below and write down some brief answers. Then write an answer to the question, 'Why do you think this cartoon was published in 1830?'

● **SOURCE 4**

Come move on there – its time you was in bed young woman
any body with half an eye could see you were in liquor

A cartoon about the police force, published in May 1830.

- Look at the policeman – what is the matter with him?
- Why has the artist drawn him talking to a water pump?
- Why is the policeman saying to the water pump 'Come move on there – its time you was in bed young woman, any body with half an eye could see you were in liquor'?
- Does the date matter? What was going on around this time that was connected with the police?
- What is the overall impression about the police that you get from the cartoon – efficient, useless, drunk, helpful, professional, stupid – or something else?

Photographs

Some students think that photographs must show the truth because they show something that was really there. This seems to make sense, but is sometimes wrong.

● **SOURCE 5**

● **SOURCE 6**

Sometimes photographs can be set up. A photographer might ask people to do something and then take a photograph of them. Sometimes a photograph can even be faked, although this is rare. In all cases the photographer will have made a deliberate decision to take a particular photograph, and as historians we need to ask why he or she did that.

The two photographs on the left are good examples of how photographs can be useful, but can also give us problems. Source 5 is a photograph of suffragettes demonstrating on a boat on the River Thames opposite the House of Commons in 1908. Source 6 is a photograph of a Liberal MP's house that was attacked by suffragette arsonists in 1913.

Both photographs are genuine – they show events that actually happened. Each tells us something about the methods used by the suffragettes.

But think a minute – why were these photographs taken? The photographers must have deliberately gone and taken these particular shots. Why? Part of the answer is no doubt to simply show people what was happening. But consider the following questions.

- Do these two photographs give similar impressions of the suffragettes? Which one shows they had a sense of humour? Which one shows they were dangerous and threatened the lives of people?
- Does the fact that they give such different impressions of the suffragettes mean that one of them is misleading or wrong? Consider carefully the dates of the two sources.
- Which photograph would a newspaper that was against the idea of votes for women be more likely to use?

These questions raise important points about photographs.

- They can only show what was happening at one moment in time and they might not be representative of the suffragettes generally.
- It is important how photographs are used by, for example, newspapers. These photographs could be used to create certain impressions of the suffragettes.

So be careful with photographs. They can be very useful, but they have to be used with caution.

Objects and artefacts

The cartoons and photographs we have been looking at were deliberately created to tell people something about crime and punishment. Other sources that we use have been left from the past just by accident. They are things that simply existed at the time, for example the skulls of people who lived in the past, or objects they made in their everyday lives. They were not made deliberately to tell us things, but we can still learn a lot from them.

Look at this photograph. The object it shows comes from a door at Durham Cathedral. Discuss with a partner what you think it is and what it has to do with crime and punishment! Look at it carefully. Look for clues and remember what you have learned about medieval criminals wanting to reach a church.

● **SOURCE 7**

You probably worked out that the object is a door knocker.

- Is it just an ordinary door knocker?
- Who or what is the face meant to represent?
- Why is it designed in this way?
- Why is this door knocker on the door of a church?

Have you come up with an answer similar to this?

The door knocker is a sanctuary knocker. A criminal on the run and looking for sanctuary would hammer on the knocker. The watchmen, who were stationed above the porch, would let him in. Once inside the church the criminal would be safe from being arrested. He had 40 days to decide whether to stand trial or to leave the country. The face, which might be the Devil, could stand for all the crimes that the criminal will be leaving outside when he enters the church. While in the church he was expected to repent of his sins.

You probably got quite close to this explanation by using your knowledge of sanctuary in the Middle Ages.

Written sources

You might think, by now, that written sources are easier to use than pictures or objects. With the latter there is quite a lot of working out to do, but surely written sources simply mean what they say? Unfortunately, this is often not the case and we also have to do a lot of work to make sense of written sources.

Read the source that follows. It is part of an unsigned letter that was delivered to Lord Monteagle at his London home by a disguised messenger on the night of 26 October 1605. The words have been modernised.

● SOURCE 8

My Lord, out of the love I feel for some of your friends, I care for your safety. Therefore I would advise you, as you value your life, to make up some excuse for not attending this Parliament. Do not ignore this warning, but go back into the country where you may await the event in safety. For though there is no appearance yet of any trouble, still I say they shall receive a terrible blow this Parliament; and they shall not see who hurts them.

Lord Monteagle took this letter to King James' chief minister Robert Cecil. A few days later, on 5 November several Catholics, including Guy Fawkes, were caught red-handed with barrels of gunpowder in a cellar next to the Houses of Parliament. What a lucky break for the king and how very public-spirited of Lord Monteagle you might think!

Here are a few facts about Lord Monteagle – he was a rather mysterious character. They will make you look at the letter in a different way.

He was friendly with several of the Catholics who were arrested. He had been arrested for his part in a rebellion against Queen Elizabeth I in 1601 but was let off surprisingly lightly. Many of the other plotters were executed. Yet by the time James became king in 1603, Monteagle seems to have become a loyal subject. The letter was delivered to Monteagle on 26 October. This was the only night that year that he stayed at his London house – what a stroke of luck!

Are you becoming a bit suspicious about the letter? Remember, the letter was not signed and the messenger who brought it was in disguise.

And here is another thing – the King's chief minister, Robert Cecil, was looking for an excuse to persecute Catholics more harshly. Some people at the time thought that he set the plot up himself to discredit Catholics. After the plot was discovered laws were passed that persecuted Catholics much more harshly than before. And remember the cellar where the plotters and the gunpowder were found? Well, this cellar was rented to the plotters by a man who worked for the government and was a friend of Cecil.

Now answer this question.

• Do you trust Lord Monteagle and the letter he says was sent?

If he did make the letter up, does this make the letter useless to historians like us? No, it doesn't. Many students make the mistake in exams of saying that biased or unreliable sources are of no use. *Never write this*. Assume that Monteagle did make the letter up. Write down what we can still learn from it.

Luckily, not all written sources are as tricky as Monteagle's letter. Read this source from the eighteenth century. It is about smuggling in a village in Cornwall.

● **SOURCE 9**

In going down the hill we met several women whose appearance was so grotesque that I could not imagine how they had altered their natural appearance. We found out that they were smugglers of liquor which they were carrying in cows' bladders fastened under their petticoats. They were so heavily laden, that it was with great difficulty that they waddled along.

Smuggling is carried on without the least worry of getting caught and without any interruptions from the Customs Officers. Smuggling seems to be a popular trade among the lower orders of people – and some hundreds gain their livelihood by it.

You can learn lots from this source about smuggling and not just the obvious things such as women smuggled liquor under their petticoats. Write down the answers to these questions and see what you have learned. Explain each answer using the evidence in the source.

- How did the author know the women were smugglers?
- Was the author surprised that the smugglers were not caught?
- Was smuggling important in this part of Cornwall?
- Was smuggling regarded as a crime by most of the people in this part of Cornwall?

What kinds of questions will you get in the exam?

There are four main types of question that can be set on sources.

1 Questions about what sources say

These questions test how well you can work out what a source says. They can be asked in different ways, for example:

What is the message of this source?

What does the author think about . . .?

What can you learn from this source about . . .?

How far do these two sources agree?

What impression does this source give of . . .?

Go back to the answer you wrote to the question on page 4, 'What message did the artist want to give criminals about dissection?' This was about the drawing showing a dissection. Compare your answer to the four opposite. Rate the answers (including yours) from 1 to 5, making 5 the best answer.

REMEMBER

- Study the source carefully and go beyond its surface meaning. Look at what the author or artist is implying or suggesting, or even what he is telling us about himself without realising.
- Explain your answer using details in the source.
- Your knowledge of the topic will help you work out what the source is saying and help you explain this in your answer.

- Only use knowledge in your answer if it helps you explain the meaning of the source. Do not tell the examiner everything you know about the topic for its own sake – they will not be impressed.
- Only do what the question asks and no more. This type of question does not ask you to say if you trust the source, so do not comment on this.

Student A

The artist is warning criminals that if they commit crimes they might be dissected. The artist does this by showing a dissection being carried out. It shows how horrible dissections were. This is a warning to criminals to stop committing crimes otherwise this might happen to them.

Student B

The artist was trying to say to criminals that surgeons were horrible, cruel people. The poor criminal who is being operated on is in great pain and the surgeons seem to be making a joke of the whole thing. You can see this by the look on their faces – they are enjoying it. One of the surgeons seems to be cutting the criminal's eye out. This will not do him any good. Nor will the dog who is eating bits of the criminal. He must be in great pain.

Student C

This drawing is a warning to criminals about what might happen to them if they continue to commit crimes. The artist has drawn lots of disgusting details to make criminals really worried about having their bodies dissected. You would think that the surgeons would have some respect for the corpse but they are letting a dog eat some of the innards. The whole thing looks like a piece of entertainment with people enjoying the dissection. This makes the whole thing humiliating for the person being dissected and for his family. In those days dissection was regarded as worse than death. People believed that they could not go to heaven if their bodies had been cut up like this.

The artist has the corpse sitting up a little to make it look as if it is alive. This was to play on the fears people had that surgeons sometimes dissected people who had not died on the scaffold and were still alive. This would make the criminals even more worried – they might be dissected when they were still alive!

Student D

Many people in those days were horrified by dissection. This happened to some criminals after they had been executed. Every year a certain number of bodies of hanged criminals were handed over to the Company of Surgeons. Surgeons would cut the bodies up. They did this to help teach medical students about different parts of the body. This was a very useful way for them to get bodies.

Examiner's comments

Answer D is the weakest answer because it completely ignores the source. It tells us something about dissections and why they were carried out, but it does not answer the question.

Answer B is also weak because it has misunderstood the source. The student who wrote it seems to think the drawing shows a criminal being operated on! However, the student has used some of the details in the drawing to show how the artist has made it all look horrible and so some marks would be awarded.

Answer A is quite good about what the artist was trying to say to criminals but the answer is not supported. To get good marks, answers should be supported by reference to details in the source and to some knowledge. This answer has neither.

Answer C is the best. Here the student does what Student A failed to do. He or she has supported their answer with reference to details in the source and to some knowledge. The details of the source have been used very well to explain the answer.

2 Questions about what you can work out from a source

These questions test whether you can use the source to work out things that go beyond what the source actually says. It is possible to work out from a source the following:

What the purpose of the artist/author was.

Why it was published at a particular time.

What kind of person might have produced the source, for example an opponent or a supporter of prison reform in the nineteenth century.

How people at the time might have reacted to the source.

Who the source was directed at (the intended audience).

Come move on there— its time you was in bed young woman any body with half an eye could see you were in liquor

Earlier, you wrote about this cartoon of a policeman talking to a water pump (page 5) and worked out why it was published in 1830.

Compare your answer to the two opposite. The good features of Answer A have been explained.

Straight to why 1830 – knowledge of Peel setting up the first police force used.

Answer A

This cartoon was published in 1830 because Robert Peel had just set up the first police force in 1829. This was the Metropolitan Police Force in London. At first there was a lot of opposition to the idea of a police force. One of the reasons for this was that people thought the recruits were of too low a quality and would not be able to do the job properly. Drunkenness was a great problem in the early years. Many of the first policemen appointed had to be sacked because they were drunk on duty. This cartoon is making this point about the first policemen. It shows a policeman drunk. We know this because he is talking to a water pump as if it was a young lady. He is even accusing the water pump of being drunk. He also has a very red face. All these details show how drunk the policeman is and get across the message that this is what the new police force is like. It will be useless. It can't do its job if all the policemen are as useless as this one.

Knowledge of people's worries about the new police force is used. It is linked to details in the cartoon, such as why the policeman is shown talking to a water pump.

Purpose of cartoon explained – the explanation grows out of the earlier parts of the answer about people's fears of the new force and why this policeman is shown as drunk. Both details of the cartoon and knowledge of the period have been used.

Answer B

This cartoon was published in 1830 because the artist is against the police. At that time lots of people were against the police force. Some thought that it was a danger to people's freedoms. They thought it would spy on people and would cost a lot of money. This would put the rates up. Some people thought that the police were useless. They said that the people who were recruited were not educated and were of poor quality. This was because they were not paid enough to attract good recruits. In the first few years drunkenness was a major problem and was the reason why many policemen were sacked.

Have a close look at Answer B. Does it:

- explain why it was published in 1830?
- explain the purpose of the cartoon?
- use details of the cartoon in its explanation?
- use some knowledge in its explanation?
- give a better or worse answer than Answer A? Give two reasons.

Now ask these questions about the answer you wrote.

3 Questions asking you to evaluate sources

These questions sometimes ask you to evaluate sources for reliability, for example:

Do you trust what a source says?

If two sources disagree, does this mean one of them cannot be trusted?

Does the content of one source make another source reliable or unreliable?

Is one source more reliable than another?

and sometimes for usefulness, for example:

In what ways is a source useful to us with reference to a particular topic?

Is one source more useful than another?

Because a source is biased, does this mean it is of no use to us?

Here are some **dos** and **don'ts** when answering these types of questions.

Reliability questions

Don't...

Claim that a source is reliable simply because of what type of source it is. For example, never write that a source is reliable because it was written at the time, or because it was written by an eyewitness, or because it was written by a vicar and all vicars can be trusted. Some sources written at the time can be trusted, others cannot. It all depends on the particular source in front of you and on what it says and why it was produced.

Do...

Look at what the source says, and at who wrote or drew it.

Check claims made in the source against your knowledge of the topic. This might help you decide if it can be trusted or not. Explain this fully, for example explain how knowledge that you have conflicts with claims made in the source.

Ask yourself – did the author or artist have any reason for writing or drawing what they did? Did they have a purpose, were they trying to influence the views of others, did they have something to cover up, or did they have something to gain? In other words, are there any reasons why you should be suspicious about what they are telling us? Sometimes you will know something about the author or artist, sometimes you will be told something about them (like you were about Lord Monteagle). Finally, make sure you explain your answer fully.

Usefulness questions

Don't...

Think that a source cannot be useful to you because it is biased. The fact that it is biased means it will tell you a lot about the person who wrote or drew it!

Assume that it is only useful for the obvious information it gives you.

Do...

Look at what the source says. The source will certainly tell you something about the views and purpose of the author or artist.

Look out for things the author or artist did not intend to tell us.

You answered a question earlier (page 8) about whether you trusted Lord Monteagle and the letter he claimed he was sent. Here are three different answers to that question. Which is the best one, and what is wrong with the other two?

Student A

I trust Lord Monteagle because he was a very important man and he would know what was going on. He was a loyal subject of the King. This proves that Lord Monteagle can be trusted. He saved the government a lot by showing them the letter.

Student B

I think Lord Monteagle was telling the truth. The letter that was sent to him tells him to go to the country and not to attend Parliament. This was a warning from one of the plotters who did not want Monteagle to get hurt when Parliament was blown up. The letter was right because a few days later the plotters were caught in a cellar with gunpowder ready to blow Parliament up.

Student C

I am not sure that I trust Lord Monteagle. He is a very shady character and was probably in the pay of the government. It is strange that he was let off so lightly when he was caught rebelling against Queen Elizabeth. Perhaps the government was blackmailing him to be an informer. It is also strange that the letter happened to be delivered on the one day that Monteagle was at home. What a coincidence. We know that Robert Cecil wanted an excuse to persecute Catholics. The letter and the catching of the plotters gave him the excuse he needed. I think Monteagle was made by Cecil to pretend the letter was delivered to him. It could be that the letter was written by Monteagle, or someone in the government, to discredit Catholics. However, the letter might be genuine. Monteagle's old friends were plotters and they might have wanted to save him from the explosion at Parliament.

See if you agree with these comments.

Student A trusts what Lord Monteagle says simply because he was an important person. The student ignores all the other things we know about Monteagle. The fact that he was an important man does not mean he was telling the truth.

Student B's answer is a bit better because he or she does use some of the evidence in the source. The student argues that the letter and Monteagle can both be trusted because the letter warns about a plot against Parliament and a few days later the plotters are caught. This answer also correctly states that Monteagle was a friend of some of the plotters and so they had a good reason for warning him not to go to Parliament. However, the problem with this answer is that it accepts the letter at face value and ignores all the other things we know about Monteagle and Robert Cecil.

Student C has written the best answer. He or she has explained the possibility that Monteagle had reasons of his own to make up the letter. The student also explains that Robert Cecil badly wanted an excuse to persecute Catholics. This all casts doubt over whether Monteagle can be trusted. However, what is particularly good about this answer is that the student does not automatically assume that Monteagle made the letter up. This possibility is explained, but the student also gives reasons why the letter might be genuine.

4 Questions asking you to use all the sources to reach an overall conclusion

There is nearly always one of these questions at the end of the exam paper. You will find one at the end of most of the source investigations that come later in this book. Here is such a question from one of those investigations:

Study all the sources. 'The witch-hunting craze of the sixteenth and seventeenth centuries was nothing more than mass hysteria directed at vulnerable women.' How far do the sources support this view? Use the sources and your knowledge to explain your answer.

If you know what to do you can pick up a lot of marks in this question (it always carries more marks than any of the other questions).

Here is what to do:

1 You must base your answer on a discussion of the sources. Do not answer the question by ignoring the sources and writing down everything you know about witches.

2 Go through all the sources quickly and make a rough list of the sources that support the statement, and a list of those that disagree with the statement. You can list the sources by letter.

3 State which sources support the statement. Explain how they do this. Refer to any source you use by letter so the examiner knows which source you are using.

The three most important things you need to remember about answering source questions are:

- All the questions will be questions about the sources – you must base your answers on the sources.
- Use your knowledge in your answer, but only use it when it helps you to say something better about the sources. Do not put it in for its own sake.
- For every source, ask yourself – why was this source produced? What was the artist or the author trying to do?

Good luck with the exam. After doing all this you should find it easy!

6 To get full marks you have to show that some sources can or cannot be trusted, in other words you should evaluate some of them. For example, there might be some sources that seem to support the statement but you do not trust them. This means they cannot really be used to support the statement. You need to explain why you do not trust them. This might mean repeating something you have written in an earlier answer — do not worry about this.

4 State which sources disagree with the statement. Explain how they do this. Refer to the sources by letter.

5 You do not have to use all the sources, but you should use most of them.

Part 2 Source investigations

Were the Middle Ages lawless?

Read all the sources, then answer the questions on page 21.

During the Middle Ages the king and his government tried to bring law and order to the country. Trial by battle was added to trial by ordeal to discover whether the accused was innocent or guilty. Later in the Middle Ages, more use was made of juries. At first these were used to report anyone suspected of crimes, and later to decide whether people were innocent or guilty. The king's judges extended justice across the country by visiting each county and holding regular courts. However, there were still many problems, such as the misuse of sanctuary and the activities of outlaws. How effective were law and order in the Middle Ages?

● SOURCE A

In the Northumberland records of 1279, seventy-two murders are listed and eighty-one culprits are identified. Of these no more than three were hanged. Six escaped to sanctuary, one was imprisoned, one fined, one pleaded benefit of clergy and sixty-nine escaped altogether.

In 1348 there were eighty-eight known cases of murder in Yorkshire, whose population was probably about the same as that of Sheffield today. If murders were committed on this scale now, there would be 10,000 a year in England and Wales instead of the average of between 500 and 600.

From a recent history book.

● SOURCE B

A medieval illustration of trial by hot iron.

● **SOURCE C**

A drawing of trial by battle.

● **SOURCE D**

King Henry has announced that, for the preservation of peace, declarations shall be made by twelve men of a hundred, to reply truthfully to this question – whether anyone, within their hundred, has been accused or suspected of robbery, murder or theft.

The creation of juries of presentment from the 'Assize of Clarendon', 1166.

● **SOURCE E**

Clause 1

Robberies, murders and acts of arson are now daily happenings and are occurring with greater frequency than ever before. Juries allow crimes to go unpunished because those responsible for the crimes are people of their own district and there is no punishment if juries conceal anything or are lax in their duty. Our Lord the king has therefore established a punishment for juries who in future conceal crimes or allow criminals to go unpunished.

Clause 5

The highways leading from one town to another shall be widened. Where there are trees or hedges, or ditches within a distance of 200 feet on either side of the highway, they shall be removed.

Clause 6

Every man shall have weapons and equipment in his house to keep the peace.

Extracts from the Statute of Winchester, 1285. This law, issued by Edward I, contained major reforms to the system of law and order in England.

WARNER BROS. *present* "THE ADVENTURES OF **ROBIN HOOD**"
with **ERROL FLYNN** OLIVIA De HAVILLAND BASIL RATHBONE CLAUDE RAINS
A WARNER BROS. PICTURE COLOUR BY TECHNICOLOR

● **SOURCE F**

A scene from a film made in the 1930s about Robin Hood. Here he is fighting against those who were trying to replace Richard I as king with his brother John.

● **SOURCE G**

For coming armed, with others, to Wysemarfelde and lying in wait to kill Robert Doufbiggying, a forester of the Duke of Lancaster, in the forest of Knaresborough, and assaulting him and John of Denton and William Forster and murdering them, so that the Duke lost their services and the forest was robbed of wood to the value of £40 and many deer.

Some of the charges brought against the outlaw John Stuffe, from court records of the 1390s.

● **SOURCE H**

John Walsh is arrested for the death of Richard Cous. The jurors say on their oath that there was an argument between John and Richard and that they were using insulting language when Richard drew a knife and threatened to wound John. John fled into an angle between two walls. Seeing no escape John drew his sword in self-defence. Richard ran towards John with his knife outstretched in order to kill John but he ran into John's sword which entered his body. He died of the wound at once. The jurors say that John could not have avoided death in any other way than by drawing his sword. He is returned to prison to await the king's pardon.

Extract from records of the king's court in Norfolk around 1310.

● **SOURCE I**

A wicked man murdered a widow in her bed in the suburbs of London. He carried away all the money she had and took sanctuary in the holy church of St George. He finally agreed to leave the church in return for permission to leave the country. As he left, he passed near the place where he had committed murder. There the women of the area came out to meet him with stones and dung and they stoned him to death.

From a fifteenth-century chronicle.

Questions

1 Study **Source A**.
What impression does this source give of law and order in the Middle Ages?
Use the source to explain your answer. [6]

2 Study **Sources B, C** and **D**.
How similar are the events in these three sources?
Use the sources and your knowledge to explain your answer. [8]

3 Study **Source E**.
What can you learn from this source about law and order in the Middle Ages?
Use the source and your knowledge to explain your answer. [9]

4 Study **Sources F** and **G**.
Do these two sources give a similar impression of medieval outlaws?
Use the sources to explain your answer. [8]

5 Study **Sources H** and **I**.
How far do these two sources prove that law and order was getting worse towards the end of the Middle Ages?
Use the sources to explain your answer. [7]

6 Study **all** the sources.
Do these sources show that the Middle Ages were lawless?
Use the sources and your knowledge to explain your answer. [12]

What can Robin Hood tell us about outlaws?

Read all the sources, then answer the questions on page 24.

Stories about Robin Hood and his band of outlaws were first written down in the 1400s, but before then they were spread by word of mouth. The places mentioned in the stories were real: the towns of Nottingham and Wakefield, and the great royal forests of Sherwood and Barnsdale that surrounded them. But it is not very likely that there was one historical Robin Hood. It is more likely that the name 'Robin Hood' was given to a number of different outlaw leaders when stories were told about them.

What is certain is that there were outlaws in medieval times. An outlaw was someone who was declared to be beyond the protection of the law. This might be, for example, because they didn't turn up in court to be tried for alleged offences. People became outlaws for a variety of different reasons. Some were fleeing from the law; others believed that law and order had broken down and they could not get justice in the law courts. There was no police force to hunt down criminals. This meant that outlaws could live in some safety in the wilder and more remote parts of England, such as Barnsdale and Sherwood forests.

● SOURCE A

On 7ᵗʰ July 1277 the Steward of the Forest found Robert the Monk and Robert of Alfreton with bows and arrows. He arrested them and took them to Blidworth and put them in prison. Later that night twenty men, armed with bows and arrows, broke down the entrance to the prison and released them. Then they attacked the Steward's house. All these men had entered the forest to kill deer.

A report from a jury of foresters to the Justices of Sherwood Forest.

● SOURCE B

John of Braythewell entered many times with force and arms the wood of the lord in Holnefryth and killed, took and carried away the wild animals belonging to the lord. He assaulted, shot at and wounded the lord's men when they tried to stop him. Therefore let him be taken.

Richard de Windhill was taken as a suspected thief because he came with a message from several thieves to the wife of the late William de Stodlay. They were begging for food. Richard de Windhill threatened to burn her unless she gave him food and money. He fled when the earl's foresters tried to capture him.

Extracts from the court records of the manor of Wakefield, 1315–16.

● SOURCE C

He [King William I 1066–1087] made many deer parks, and he established laws about them. These laws said that whoever slew a hart, or a hind, should be deprived of his eyesight. He forbade men to kill the boars as well. He loved the tall deer as if he were their father. Likewise he decreed that the hares should go free. Rich men complained and poor men shuddered at these new laws.

From the *Anglo-Saxon Chronicle*. This was a history of England written by monks between about 891 and 1154.

● **SOURCE D**

William de Marisco being dragged to a gibbet. Accused of killing Richard, Earl Marshal, in 1234, he was outlawed, captured and executed in 1242. After being dragged behind the horse, he was hanged, disembowelled and cut into four pieces, which were displayed in four cities.

● **SOURCE E**

Out of their lying mouths, evil people have indicted me
Of wicked robberies and other crimes.
Because of this, I do not dare to visit my friends.

If these wicked jurors refuse to mend their ways
So that I may ride about freely,
I'll make their heads fly off if I can capture them.

You who are indicted, I advise you, come with me,
To the green wood of Belregard, where there is no entanglement,
Just wild animals and pleasant shade;
For the common law is too unreliable.

A poet, writing in about 1306, explains why he became an outlaw.

● **SOURCE F**

But Robin pulled out a two-handed sword
That hanged down by his knee
There where the sheriff and his men stood thickest
Towards them went he.

Twice he ran his sword right through them,
In truth I to you say.
He wounded many a mother's son
And twelve he killed that day.

Much did the same to the little page
For fear that he would tell.

From one of the oldest stories of Robin Hood, *Robin Hood and the Monk*. It is thought to date from the 1330s. Robin is spotted by a monk whom he has earlier robbed. The monk raises a hue and cry and the Sheriff of Nottingham and his men try to catch Robin. Little John kills the monk and Much kills the pageboy.

● **SOURCE G**

Attend and listen, gentlemen, who are of freeborn blood. I shall tell you about a good yeoman whose name is Robin Hood. While he was alive, he was a proud outlaw, and no outlaw was found who was so polite. Robin lived in Barnsdale with the good yeoman Little John, Will Scarlock, and Much the Miller's son.

Then said Little John, "Master, tell us where we shall go, what life we shall lead? What shall we take and what shall we leave behind? Where shall we rob? Who shall we beat and tie up?"

Then said Robin, "Look that you do no harm to any small farmer who tills with his plough. Nor shall you harm any good yeoman who walks by the greenwood thicket, or a knight or a squire for they are good fellows. However, you should beat and tie up bishops and archbishops, and don't forget the Sheriff of Nottingham."

From *The Gest of Robyn Hode*. It probably started as a ballad, sung by minstrels, and was first written down in the 1400s.

● **SOURCE H**

Then lived the famous murderer, Robert Hood, as well as Little John, together with their accomplices from among those who had lost their land and been outlawed, whom the foolish common people are so very fond of celebrating in comedy and tragedy.

From a *Chronicle* written by Walter Bower in about 1440. Here he is writing about the year 1266.

● **SOURCE I**

An early portrait of Robin Hood, drawn sometime between 1510 and 1515.

● **SOURCE J**

About the time when Richard I was imprisoned in Germany [1192–9] the notorious robbers, Robin Hood and Little John, lurked in the woods, stealing the goods only of rich men. They killed nobody except those who attacked them, or offered resistance when defending their property. Robin, from what he had stolen, could afford to employ a hundred archers. They were so skilful at fighting that four hundred brave men were afraid to attack them. Robin would not allow women to be mistreated and never robbed the poor, but rather helped them by giving them some of the wealth taken from the abbots. The robberies of this man I condemn, but of all robbers he was the most humane and the chief. The exploits of Robert are celebrated in songs throughout all Britain.

From the *History of Greater Britain*, written by John Major in 1521.

● **SOURCE K**

Gangs of outlaws were feared. They stole from anyone, including villagers. They threatened their victims with arson, extorting money or goods in return for not burning homes down. Outlaws regularly used violence. Around 10 per cent of murder victims were killed during robberies, usually by these outlaws. These crimes explain why juries found violent robbers guilty and were glad to see them hang. Juries did not find excuses for them that they did for fellow villagers, even those accused of murder. Ordinary people had little sympathy for outlaws.

From *Crime and Punishment through Time* by Ian Dawson, published in 1999.

Questions

1 Study **Sources A** and **B**.
Do you agree that it was dangerous to live in Barnsdale or Sherwood at this time?
Use the sources to explain your answer. **[5]**

2 Study **Sources A, B** and **C**.
How far does the *Anglo-Saxon Chronicle* (Source C) explain what was happening in Sources A and B?
Use the sources and your knowledge to explain your answer. **[6]**

3 Study **Sources D** and **E**.
Source D shows the dreadful consequences of becoming an outlaw. Why, then, did the poet (Source E) take the risk?
Use the sources and your knowledge to explain your answer. **[7]**

4 Study **Sources F** and **G**.
Do you think these stories are about the same 'Robin Hood'?
Use the sources and your knowledge to explain your answer. **[7]**

5 Study **Sources F, G, H** and **I**.
Why did people draw pictures, sing songs and tell tales about child murderers, killers and thieves?
Use the sources and your knowledge to explain your answer. **[8]**

6 Study **Sources J** and **K**.
When Source K says that ordinary people had little sympathy for outlaws, does it prove that Source J is wrong?
Use the sources to explain your answer. **[7]**

7 Study **all** the sources.
'The stories of Robin Hood tell us nothing at all about real outlaws.'
How far do the sources support this statement?
Use the sources and your knowledge to explain your answer. **[10]**

Why was there a witch-hunting craze in the sixteenth and seventeenth centuries?

Read all the sources, then answer the questions on page 28.

Witchcraft, or doing the Devil's work, had always been a crime. However, until the 1500s it was regarded as a minor crime and was usually dealt with in the Church courts. Indeed, between 1066 and 1500 no more than a dozen witches were hanged, and these were usually involved in plots against the monarch or his friends. Then everything seemed to change. In 1542, Parliament passed a law that said witchcraft was a felony punishable by death. Twenty-one years later, another Act listed different kinds of witchcraft and in 1604 the earlier Acts were brought together.

For hundreds of years, ordinary people had found local 'wise women' very useful. They used herbs and spells to, for example, cure illness and protect against early death; to bring about a good harvest; to find lost children, and cause two people to fall in love. Then the witch-hunts began. Prosecutions for witchcraft reached a peak in Elizabeth I's reign (1558–1603) and again during the civil wars of the 1640s. Hundreds of witches were hanged, and for every case that came to court there were many more that stayed as accusations at village level. Witch-hunts were common and were often hysterical, making it impossible for those accused to find justice.

● SOURCE A

I am poor and I could not pay Ursula Kemp. She asked for cheese as payment but I had none to give her. She murmured that she would get even with me. Soon afterwards I began to limp.

Ursula and I had a little matter of business between us, but I did not keep my side of the bargain, knowing Ursula to be a naughty beast. So Ursula, in revenge, bewitched my child. I have proof that it was Ursula who had so hurt my babe. When the child was no more than one year old, I carried her past Ursula's house and the child cried "Wo, wo" and pointed its finger to Ursula's window.

These two witness statements, made under oath, come from the trial of Ursula Kemp. She was one of 13 women from the village of St Osyth, in Essex, who were accused of witchcraft in 1582.

● SOURCE B

Yes, I had the four imps my son has told of. Two of them, Tilly and Jack, were 'hees' whose job was to kill people. Two, Tiffin and Piggin, were 'shes' who punished, made people lame and destroyed goods and cattle. I confess that I killed my brother's wife. And Grace Thurlow's child. I made it fall out of its cradle and break its neck. I bewitched the little babe of Annie Letherdall.

Ursula Kemp first of all said she was innocent. Then, after a long trial, during which her eight-year-old son testified against her, she made this confession.

● SOURCE C

There are so many of these detestable slaves of the Devil at this time and in this country. Because of this I have been encouraged to write this book. I want to convince the doubting hearts of many people of two things: that assaults by Satan are carried out by witches and that the guilty should be punished.

From a book called *Demonologie* written by King James VI of Scotland in 1597, six years before he became King James I of England.

● **SOURCE D**

● **SOURCE F**

He laid her body naked to the waist, with her clothes over her head. With fright and shame all her blood ran to one part of her body. He pushed a pin into her thigh, and suddenly let her clothes fall and asked her why she did not bleed. Then he took out the pin and set her aside, calling her a child of the devil.

Part of a contemporary account of the examination of a witch at her trial in Newcastle in 1649.

The public hanging of three witches in Chelmsford, Essex, in 1589. The women, Joan Prentice, Joan Cony and Joan Upney, are shown here with their 'familiars' (demons who obeyed witches and often appeared as small animals).

● **SOURCE E**

A contemporary engraving showing the trial of Mary Sutton in 1612, who was accused of being a witch. The people who accused her said that if she was innocent she would sink and if she floated, she was guilty.

● **SOURCE G**

County	No. of accusations 1560–1700	No. of executions 1560–1700
Sussex	33	1
Surrey	71	5
Hertfordshire	81	8
Kent	132	16
Essex	473 (50 of these were the work of Matthew Hopkins in 1645)	82
Total	790	112 (Altogether about 1000 witches were executed in 200 years)

This chart shows the number of witchcraft trials in south-east England 1560–1700.

● **SOURCE H**

● **SOURCE I**

I know that Matthew Hopkins intends to come here to search for witches. I do not want him anywhere near my parish. If I let him in, then every old woman with a wrinkled face, a furrowed brow, a hairy lip, a crooked tooth or a squint eye, and who speaks with a squeaking voice or a scolding tongue will be called a witch.

From a pamphlet written by the Rev John Gaule in 1646. He was the vicar of Huntingdon.

In this contemporary illustration, Matthew Hopkins is shown discovering two witches. The women are talking to their evil spirits, called 'familiars'. Matthew Hopkins, a lawyer, appointed himself 'Witch-Finder General'. His cruel methods led to hundreds of women in the south-east of England, particularly in Essex, confessing to being witches. He was himself hanged for witchcraft in August 1647.

● **SOURCE J**

Towards the middle of the 1600s, witch-hunts became much more hysterical than they had in the past. Many judges complained about the vindictiveness with which they were pursued. Lord Chief Justice Sir John Holt, for example, seemed not to believe in witchery at all, and did his best to bring about acquittals. However, there were others who seemed determined to secure convictions even on the flimsiest of evidence. Lord Chief Justice North confessed that he had allowed the conviction of three innocent women at Exeter because he feared that acquittal might result in a fresh wave of witch-hunting.

From C Hibbert, *The English,* published in 1994.

Questions

1 Study **Source A**.
Why were people ready to believe 'evidence' like this?
Use the source and your knowledge to explain your answer.   [5]

2 Study **Sources A** and **B**.
Do you agree that Ursula Kemp must have been a witch?
Use the sources and your knowledge to explain your answer.   [6]

3 Study **Source C**.
Are you surprised that a king should write a book about witchcraft?
Use the source and your knowledge to explain your answer.   [7]

4 Study **Sources D, E** and **F**.
These sources all show methods involved in the legal treatment of women accused of being witches. Were these women treated fairly?
Use the sources and your knowledge to explain your answer.   [8]

5 Study **Sources G** and **H**.
'A historian investigating the work of Matthew Hopkins would find Source G much more reliable than Source H.' Do you agree?
Use the sources and your knowledge to explain your answer.   [7]

6 Study **Sources I** and **J**.
Do you think that the Rev John Gaule would have agreed with Lord Chief Justice Sir John Holt, or with Lord Chief Justice North?
Use the sources to explain your answer.   [7]

7 Study **all** the sources.
'The witch-hunting craze of the sixteenth and seventeenth centuries was nothing more than mass hysteria directed at vulnerable women.'
How far do the sources support this view?
Use all the sources and your knowledge to explain your answer.   [10]

SOURCE INVESTIGATION

Why were vagabonds treated so harshly in the sixteenth century?

Read all the sources, then answer the questions on page 31.

Vagabonds were beggars and vagrants who wandered the country without a job. In the sixteenth century the authorities became very worried about them. Some of them travelled the country in large gangs. Some vagrants, such as those with disabilities, or single mothers with children, could not work and had to beg. Others genuinely wanted jobs and were not criminals. Some, probably a minority, pretended to be ill or to have disabilities as an excuse for begging, while others were criminals who attacked and robbed people. Some towns set up schemes to help those that were old, sick or unable to help themselves and to force others into work. But there was enormous alarm about vagrants and many were whipped, branded and even executed.

● **SOURCE A**

Idle beggars make corrosives and apply them to the fleshy parts of their bodies and lay ratsbane and spearwort to their healthy limbs to cause pitiful sores and move the hearts of the passers-by so they will give them large gifts.

They are all thieves. They lick the sweat from the true labourer's brow and take from the godly poor what is due to them. It is not yet sixty years since this trade began but it has prospered since that time for they are now supposed to be above 10,000 persons as I have heard reported.

From William Harrison's *Description Of England*, published in 1577.

● **SOURCE B**

An engraving from the sixteenth century showing the punishments given to beggars.

● **SOURCE C**

An engraving showing beggars from the second half of the sixteenth century.

● **SOURCE D**

An engraving showing beggars from the second half of the sixteenth century.

● **SOURCE E**

With the aim of making young people used to and brought up in labour and work so they do not grow into idle rogues. Also with the aim that those who are already grown up in idleness and so be rogues, may not have any excuse in saying they cannot get work. They shall be set to work in every city and town within this realm. Wool, hemp, iron and other stuff shall be provided.

From a law passed by Parliament in 1576.

● SOURCE F

These are the sins which make God's justice punish people with poverty.

1 Misspending their times in idleness, when they might have worked.

2 Their wasting of their goods and money in drinking.

3 Their daily complaining at others' prosperity, when they themselves have so little.

4 Their failure to attend their parish church to hear and learn their duties better.

From a pamphlet published in 1579.

● SOURCE G

Having long observed the thefts and disorder within this country where I serve and finding they multiply daily I may justly say that the great numbers of idle, wandering people and robbers of the land are the main cause of the problem. They do not work and yet spend double as much as the labourer does for they lie idly in alehouses day and night eating and drinking excessively.

The most dangerous are the wandering soldiers and other stout rogues of which there are three or four hundred in the county. They grow more dangerous in that they have spread fear among the Justices of the Peace. Recently a very sturdy rogue was brought to court and ordered to be whipped. He swore a great oath that if he was whipped it should be the dearest whipping that some there in the court had ever had. This put such fear into the JP that the prisoner was not whipped or harmed in any way.

From a letter to the government from Edward Hext, a Justice of the Peace in Somerset. The letter was written in 1596 at a time of very poor harvests.

Questions

1 Study **Source A**.
Why do you think Harrison was worried about vagrants?
Use the source and your knowledge to explain your answer.   [7]

2 Study **Source B**.
Are you surprised by this source?
Use the source and your knowledge to explain your answer.   [7]

3 Study **Sources C** and **D**.
Do you think these two engravings were published for the same reason?
Use the sources and your knowledge to explain your answer.   [7]

4 Study **Sources E** and **F**.
How far would the author of Source E have agreed with the author of Source F?
Use the sources and your knowledge to explain your answer.   [8]

5 Study **Source G**.
Why did Hext write this letter?
Use the source and your knowledge to explain your answer.   [9]

6 Study **all** the sources.
'Vagrants were treated harshly because people in the sixteenth century thought they were pretending not to be able to work.' How far do the sources support this statement?
Use the sources and your knowledge to explain your answer.   [12]

The Gunpowder Plot: who were the criminals?

Read all the sources, then answer the questions on page 34.

In November 1605, Robert Cecil, King James I's chief minister, revealed a terrible plot. A group of Catholics, led by Robert Catesby, Francis Tresham and Thomas Percy, had decided to blow up the King and the lords when they assembled for the state opening of Parliament. They had tunnelled under the Houses of Parliament and had stacked barrels of gunpowder in a cellar. Guy Fawkes (who called himself Mr Johnson) was caught in the very act of setting light to a fuse that would ignite the gunpowder. Guy Fawkes was arrested. The other conspirators were tracked down to Holbeache House in Staffordshire. There, Catesby and Percy were killed by the same bullet; two others died in the struggle and the rest were later tried, hanged, drawn and quartered.

It seems a simple story, and it could have been true – but was it? Many people believe that Robert Cecil knew about the plot and 'discovered' it just in time, and so used it to turn people against Catholics. Others say that Robert Cecil set up the plot himself so that he could persuade Parliament to pass harsh laws against Catholics. Some say there was a plot that really was uncovered in the nick of time and that it simply proved how dangerous the Catholics were at the beginning of the seventeenth century. What do you think? Who were the Gunpowder Plot criminals?

● SOURCE A

The King's kindness has ended in this, Cecil told me. Catholic priests go openly about the country, saying mass, and this gives great offence to others. Nothing can be done. The laws must be obeyed. We cannot hope for good government while we have a large number of people who obey foreign rulers, as Catholics do. The priests preach that the Catholics must do everything to keep their religion – even if it means killing the King.

The Venetian ambassador, writing to his masters in Venice, reporting the views of Robert Cecil about Catholics. Cecil (1563–1612) was James I's chief minister, responsible for security.

● SOURCE B

It has pleased almighty God to discover the most cruel and detestable plot. The plot was to kill the King, Queen, Prince, Council, Clergy, Judges and principal gentlemen by secretly putting a great quantity of gunpowder into a cellar under Parliament and so to have blown up all in an instant. God, out of his mercy and just revenge, allowed it to be discovered.

The main plotter is one Johnson [Guy Fawkes], a Yorkshireman and servant to Thomas Percy. This Percy had, about a year and a half ago, hired a house close to Parliament, from which he had access to the cellar to store his wood and coal. He is a catholic, and so is his man Johnson. Into this cellar Johnson had carried a great quantity of powder, all of which he had cunningly covered with firewood. On Tuesday at midnight, as he was busy to prepare his things for explosion, he was caught in the place itself. There was found some fine powder, to make a fuse. He would have saved himself from the blow by about half an hour.

Part of a letter from Robert Cecil to the English ambassador in Brussels, written on 9 November 1605.

● SOURCE C

My lord
Out of the love I bear to some of your friends, I have a care of your preservation.
Therefore I would advise you, as you value your life, to devise some excuse to shift
of your attendance at this parliament, for god and man hath agreed to punish
the wickedness of this time. Do not take this warning lightly, but retire yourself
into your estates where you may expect the event in safety. I say they shall receive
a terrible blow this parliament, yet they shall not see who hurts them. This advice
is not to be condemned because it may do you good and can do you no harm.

On 26 October 1605, a mysterious stranger delivered a letter to Lord Monteagle.
It was thought to come from Francis Tresham, Monteagle's brother-in-law. Lord
Monteagle had it read out to some friends who were dining with him at the
time. He then passed it on to Robert Cecil. This is part of that letter. Some of the
words have been modernised.

● SOURCE D

If he will not otherwise
confess, the gentler
tortures are to be first
used, and then the
uttermost pain.

King James' orders about
Guy Fawkes'
interrogation after he
was arrested.

● SOURCE E

Guy Fawkes' normal signature (top) and his signature
after torture.

● SOURCE F

Catesby suggested making a mine under the upper
House of Parliament because religion had been
unjustly suppressed there. Twenty barrels of
gunpowder were moved to the cellar. It was not
intended to set fire to the fuse until the King came
into the House, and then I intended to do it so the
gunpowder might more surely blow up a quarter of
an hour later. It was agreed to seize Lady Elizabeth,
the king's eldest daughter, and to proclaim her
Queen.

Guy Fawkes was arrested on 4 November 1605. This is
part of his confession, made after torture in the
Tower of London, on 17 November 1605.

● SOURCE G

An early seventeenth-
century print of the
executions of the
gunpowder plotters.

● **SOURCE H**

Some hold it as certain that there has been foul play and that some of the government secretly spun a web to entangle these poor gentlemen.

Written by an Italian visitor to England in 1605.

● **SOURCE I**

If the Guy Fawkes case came up before the Court of Appeal today, the judges would surely acquit him.

First, no one has ever seen the attempted tunnel. Builders excavating the area in 1823 found neither a tunnel nor any rubble.

Second, the gunpowder. In 1605, the government had a monopoly on its manufacture. The government did not display the gunpowder and nobody saw it in the cellars.

Third, these cellars were let by the government to a known Catholic agitator.

Fourth, the Tresham letter. Handwriting experts agree that it was not written by Francis Tresham.

From *The Gunpowder Plot* by R Crampton, published in 1990.

Questions

1 Study **Source A**.
What does this source tell you about Robert Cecil?
Use the source to explain your answer. [5]

2 Study **Sources A** and **B**.
How far does Source B show that Robert Cecil's worries about the Catholics were correct?
Use the sources and your knowledge to explain your answer. [7]

3 Study **Source C**.
Why do you think this letter was written?
Use the source and your knowledge to explain your answer. [8]

4 Study **Sources D, E** and **F**.
Guy Fawkes' confession was made under torture.
Does this mean it cannot be trusted?
Use the sources and your knowledge to explain your answer. [6]

5 Study **Source G**.
Why do you think the plotters were punished so publicly and so savagely?
Use the source and your knowledge to explain your answer. [7]

6 Study **Sources H** and **I**.
Does Source I prove that Source H is correct in what it says about government involvement in the Gunpowder Plot?
Use the sources to explain your answer. [7]

7 Study **all** the sources.
'The real criminal in the Gunpowder Plot was Robert Cecil, not Guy Fawkes.'
How far do the sources support this view?
Use the sources and your knowledge to explain your answer. [10]

Were smugglers violent and dangerous?

Read all the sources, then answer the questions on page 37.

In the eighteenth century smuggling was common. In the hidden coves and the river estuaries of the English coast, goods were brought into the country without paying government duties (taxes). This made the goods much cheaper and therefore very attractive to many people. The government customs officers who were meant to catch the smugglers had a hopeless job – they could not possibly keep watch on all of the hundreds of miles of English coastline. When smugglers were caught they were often found not guilty by juries of local people who either supported the smugglers or had been threatened by them.

Many people regarded the smugglers as harmless and even as heroes. They thought they performed a useful service to everyone by keeping prices down. However, others saw them as dangerous and violent criminals who were depriving the government of important taxes and harming the country's economy.

● SOURCE A

Smugglers supplied huge amounts of lace, tobacco, wine, spirits and tea. Half the tea drunk in England was smuggled! Smuggling was carried out with great skill and cunning. Tobacco was made into ropes and brandy kegs were hidden in lobster pots. Once they had landed the goods the smuggling gangs were ready to fight off coastguards and mutilate customs officers and informers. However, many people did not regard smuggling as a serious crime. Smugglers were seen as romantic adventurers.

Sir Robert Walpole, the Prime Minister, used a government barge to bring his smuggled wine up the Thames. Smuggling was far too widespread for the customs officials to control it, and some customs officials were corrupt or incompetent.

An extract from a recent history book.

● SOURCE B

Smugglers are as remarkable for their skill in seamanship as for their bravery in the hour of danger. Their local knowledge has been very useful to the Navy, into which, however, they never enter, unless sent on board ships of war as a punishment for some crime committed against the customs laws. They are hardy, sober, and faithful to each other.

From a book by a captain in the Royal Navy, published in 1837.

● SOURCE C

The smuggling trade was vicious and degrading, breeding contempt for the law on the one hand and suspicion and fear on the other. The smugglers were ready to carry out any villainy that their violent natures and love of money prompted them to.

Involvement in smuggling was so widespread that for a long time smuggling seemed to be the correct course of action and indeed an honourable occupation in the face of grinding poverty and a stupid government which put the customs duties at far too high a level.

A recent description of smuggling.

● SOURCE D

The smugglers began with the customs officer Galley, cut off his nose and his private parts, broke every bone in his body and after several hours' of torture killed him. Chater, an informer, they carried to a dry well, hung him from a cross beam, leaving him to die with hunger and pain; but when they came, several days after, and heard him groan, they cut the rope, let him drop to the bottom, and threw in logs and stones to cover him. The person who gave this information in court was in disguise to prevent him from suffering the same fate.

From a newspaper report from the time of the trial of members of the Hawkhurst gang in 1748. The Hawkhurst gang were a well-known gang of smugglers in Dorset and other parts of southern England. Galley had been escorting Chater, who had identified one of the gang, to the trial.

● **SOURCE E**

An engraving, published in 1748, showing the Hawkhurst gang. Its caption reads 'The Bloody and Inhuman Smugglers throwing down stones on the dying Body of Daniel Chater, whom they had flung into Lady Holt Well.'

● **SOURCE F**

An illustration from the nineteenth century showing the Hawkhurst gang murdering Galley and Chater.

● **SOURCE G**

In going down the hill we met several women whose appearance was so grotesque that I could not imagine how they had altered their natural appearance. We found out that they were villagers who were smuggling liquor which they were carrying in cows' bladders fastened under their petticoats. They were so heavily laden, that it was with great difficulty that they waddled along.

Smuggling is carried on without the least worry of getting caught and without any interruptions from the Customs Officers. Smuggling seems to be a popular trade among the lower orders of people – and some hundreds gain their livelihood by it.

An account by a visitor to a Cornish coastal village in 1799.

● **SOURCE H**

An illustration showing villagers 'watching the wall' to make sure they do not see the smugglers go by with their contraband.

● **SOURCE I**

An illustration published in the eighteenth century called 'Smugglers alarmed'. It shows smugglers in their house while customs officials are approaching.

● **SOURCE J**

A cartoon published in 1810. The woman, pretending to be pregnant, would take the smuggled goods hidden under her dress into the local town where they would be sold.

Questions

1 Study **Source A**.
What impressions does this source give of smugglers and smuggling?
Use the source to explain your answer.   [6]

2 Study **Sources B** and **C**.
How far do these sources agree about smugglers?
Use the sources to explain your answer.   [7]

3 Study **Sources D, E** and **F**.
Does Source D prove that Source E is more reliable than Source F?
Use the sources and your knowledge to explain your answer.   [9]

4 Study **Sources G** and **H**.
Are you surprised by the actions of the villagers in Source H?
Use the sources and your knowledge to explain your answer.   [8]

5 Study **Sources I** and **J**.
How useful are these two sources for explaining why smugglers were so successful?
Use the sources and your knowledge to explain your answer.   [8]

6 Study **all** the sources.
Do these sources show that smugglers were violent and dangerous?
Use the sources and your knowledge to explain your answer.   [12]

Transportation: was it a soft punishment?

Read all the sources, then answer the questions on page 41.

Convicts were first transported to the American colonies and the West Indies. When America gained its independence, transportation had to stop. This led to British prisons becoming overcrowded and in 1787 convicts started to be transported to Australia. By 1836 75,200 convicts had been sent there.

Many of the most dangerous convicts were kept in prison settlements like those on Van Diemen's Land (now called Tasmania) while others were 'assigned' to settlers for whom they had to work in return for shelter, food and a very small sum of money (£10 a year). After serving four years of a seven-year sentence convicts could be given a ticket-of-leave. This meant that they no longer had to work as an assigned man or woman for a master. They could work for themselves but had to stay in Australia. The ticket had to be renewed each year until the sentence had been served. Many of these convicts stayed in Australia after they had served their sentences.

There were many complaints about the dreadful conditions suffered by the convicts but others claimed that conditions were too 'soft' and that convicts were being rewarded for their crimes by being sent to Australia.

● **SOURCE A**

An engraving from 1792 entitled 'Farewell to Black-eyed Sue and Sweet Poll of Plymouth'. The convicts, who are about to be transported, are saying goodbye to their lovers.

● **SOURCE B**

An illustration from 1787 entitled 'Convicts Embarking for Botany Bay'. In the background you can see the bodies of hanged criminals – the alternative to transportation.

● **SOURCE C**

A drawing from the time of convicts in Tasmania (or Van Diemen's Land as it was known then). Tasmania contained several prison settlements, all of which had terrible reputations. The convicts are carrying bundles of wooden tiles. They had to do this over a distance of 48 kilometres a day.

● **SOURCE D**

Convicts are punished to the extent of 50 to 75 lashes, solitary confinement and months, or even years, of hard labour in chains for crimes such as petty thefts and arguing among themselves. The condition of the convicts is one of unmitigated wretchedness. Several men at Norfolk Island cut the heads of their fellow prisoners with a hoe while at work, with a certainty of being executed. They acted in this way stating that they knew they would be hanged, but it was better than being where they were.

A government report describing conditions in prison settlements in Australia.

● **SOURCE E**

It is true the convicts are sent out here as punishment. But it is equally true that it is not in the interests of the master to make the convict's service a punishment but rather to make his condition as comfortable as he can afford. The interests of the master contradict the aim of transportation which is to punish the criminal.

A government official in Tasmania, 1831. The island of Tasmania (or Van Diemen's Land as it was known then) had several prison settlements which had dreadful reputations.

● **SOURCE F**

He was in the habit of putting handcuffs, and leg-irons on them, and throwing them into a dungeon on that estate where they remained for three days without meat or drink. He never went out without loaded pistols and a belt-full of handcuffs. He has drawn so much blood from the flogged backs of his assigned men, as would make him swim in human gore.

John Goodwin, a campaigner for the abolition of transportation, writing to a fellow campaigner. He is describing how a manager of one of the largest estates in Australia treated his convicts.

● **SOURCE G**

We must mention those convicts who have obtained a pardon or have become free at the end of their sentence. In this group are to be found some individuals who are very wealthy. They have land and large flocks of sheep. Most, however, are labourers and small shopkeepers; and if they work hard they have every chance of making an honest living. But of the numerous crimes committed in the colony, most are committed by this group. Among them are to be found the cattle-stealers and receivers of stolen goods.

From a government report, 1838.

● **SOURCE H**

As to my living I find it better than I ever expected thank God. As for tea and sugar I could almost swim in it. I am allowed a pound of sugar and quarter of a pound of tea per week and plenty of tobacco and good white bread and sometimes beef, sometimes mutton, sometimes pork. This I have every day. Plenty of fruit puddings and I have two suits of clothes a year. I want for nothing except for my liberty.

From a letter from a convict to his parents in Britain. He was assigned as a gardener to one of the settlers.

● **SOURCE I**

The authorities had difficulty in convincing criminals in England that Australia was a terrible place to go. There was the idea that you might be better off there than in England. This idea may have come from prisoners sending letters home playing down their sufferings to soothe the anxieties of their wives and children. Also, those prisoners who were destroyed by the system did not write home, those who prospered sometimes did.

From a book published in 1987.

TRANSPORTATION: WAS IT A SOFT PUNISHMENT? **41**

EARLY MODERN AGE   EARLY MODERN AGE 1500–1750   EARLY MODERN AGE 1500–1750   EARLY MODERN AGE 1500–1750   RLY MODERN AGE 1500–1750

● **SOURCE J**

A drawing of dogs guarding the only route of escape from the prison settlement at Port Arthur on Van Diemen's Land.

Questions

1 Study **Sources A** and **B**.
Are both of these illustrations sympathetic to the convicts?
Use the source to explain your answer.   [6]

2 Study **Sources C** and **D**.
How useful are these sources as evidence of the conditions faced by convicts in Australia?
Use the sources and your knowledge to explain your answer.   [6]

3 Study **Sources E** and **F**.
Which of these two sources do you think is the more reliable?
Use the sources and your knowledge to explain your answer.   [7]

4 Study **Source G**.
Does this source prove that transportation was a success?
Use the source and your knowledge to explain your answer.   [7]

5 Study **Sources H** and **I**.
Does Source I make Source H worthless as evidence?
Use the sources and your knowledge to explain your answer.   [8]

6 Study **Source J**.
Are you surprised by this picture?
Use the source and your knowledge to explain your answer.   [6]

7 Study **all** the sources.
How far do these sources show that transportation was a soft punishment?
Use the sources and your knowledge to explain your answer.   [10]

SOURCE INVESTIGATION 8

What was the truth about Sweeney Todd?

Read all the sources, then answer the questions on page 45.

Sweeney Todd, the Demon Barber of Fleet Street, with his famous catch-phrase 'I polish 'em off', is one of the best-known figures in the history of crime. The story tells us that Sweeney Todd was a London barber in the late eighteenth century. He used a revolving chair in his shop to tumble victims into a cellar below. Here, their throats were cut and their valuables taken. The corpses were then taken through underground passageways to Mrs Lovett's who turned them into pies to be sold in her shop. Some sources claim he murdered over 160 people!

The story became popular in the second half of the nineteenth century when various versions were published in 'penny dreadfuls'. These were cheap magazines and sold in their thousands. They were full of gruesome stories about crimes and violence. Since then there have been films and musicals about Sweeney Todd. They all give different accounts of the story. Some historians are not sure that Sweeney Todd ever existed. Others are sure but disagree about the details of the story. Is it possible to get at the truth about Sweeney Todd?

● **SOURCE A**

Possible route of tunnel

Mrs Lovett's Pie Shop

Sweeney Todd's 186 Fleet Street

Chancery Lane

Bell Yard

Fetter Lane

Hen and Chicken Court

Strand Fleet Street

St Dunstan's Church

A map of the part of London where the story is set.

● **SOURCE B**

A CUT-THROAT BARBER

A horrid murder has been committed in Fleet Street on the person of a young gentleman from the country while on a visit to relations in London.

During the course of a walk through the city, he chanced to stop to admire the striking clock of St Dunstan's Church and there fell into conversation with a man in the clothing of a barber.

The two men came to an argument, and of a sudden the barber took from his clothing a razor and slit the throat of the young man, thereafter disappearing into the alleyway of Hen and Chicken Court, and was seen no more.

From the *Daily Courant* newspaper, 14 April 1785.

● SOURCE C

It appears that for a considerable time the Church of St Dunstan's had become insufferable from a peculiar smell. The magistrate examined the vaults and found that almost every vault was full of the fresh remains of the dead. He found that into the old coffins, there had been thrust fresh bodies. The magistrate continued his investigations and found that there was an underground connection from beneath the shaving shop of the prisoner, and the cellar of a house in Bell Yard which was occupied by a female named Lovett. It will be shown in evidence that the way the larger portion of the flesh was got rid of was by converting it into meat and pork-pies on the premises of Mrs Lovett.

The words of the prosecuting lawyer in Sweeney Todd's trial in 1802 as reported in *The Newgate Calendar*, published in the early nineteenth century. *The Newgate Calendar* provided sensational accounts of murders, trials and executions and was sometimes put together from the sheets sold at public executions. One of its aims was to warn people what nasty things would happen to them if they broke the law.

● SOURCE D

I did some research in the old street directories. Despite an exhaustive search through the directories of London through the years 1768–1850, I could find no Sweeney Todd.

At first these bones [found under the cellars of 186 Fleet Street] seemed like the remains of some of Sweeney Todd's victims, but on closer investigation another possibility became apparent. The old St Dunstan's Church used to stand next door and so the bones could equally have been from the old church vaults.

From the findings of recent research into Sweeney Todd.

● SOURCE E

Towards the end of the fourteenth century
There lived a sort of demon barber,
Who slit his clients' throats at 24 Rue des Marmouzets.

He carried on this horrible trade
And nobody could resist him,
In his cellar he polished them off,
His accomplice a villainous Pie Merchant next door.

This horrid tale also tells us
That he worked with a ferocious female
Fiercer than the fiercest bailiff.

For all the poor devils he killed
His partner converted into pork pies!

From a French ballad of the fifteenth century.

● SOURCE F

There was an awful stillness in the shop and all eyes were fixed on Mrs Lovett and the opening through which the next batch of those delicious pies were coming. For a moment Mrs Lovett paused to take breath. The load seemed heavier than usual, she thought as her nerves were beginning to fail her. She began to turn the handle again. At last the tops of the pies appeared. But then up flew the trays and pies, as if something had exploded beneath them. A tall, slim man sprang out of the shaft and onto the counter.

'Gentlemen' he cried 'I am Mrs Lovett's cook. The pies are made of human flesh!'

From a 'Penny Dreadful' published in 1897. The author was anonymous.

● SOURCE G

Believing that I am on the edge of the grave, I, Margery Lovett, make this statement.

Sweeney Todd bought the houses in Fleet Street and Bell Yard. By his own exertions he excavated an underground connection between the two, mining right under St Dunstan's Church, and through the vault of that building.

When he had completed all his arrangements he came to me and made his offer. The plan he proposed was that the pie-shop should be opened for the sole purpose of getting rid of the bodies of people whom he might think proper to murder in or under his shop.

A newspaper's account of Mrs Lovett's confession to the Governor of Newgate Prison, shortly after her arrest in 1801. She committed suicide in prison a few weeks later. Her confession led to Sweeney Todd's arrest, trial and execution in 1802.

● SOURCE H

A drawing of Sweeney Todd, copies of which were on sale at the time of his trial in 1802.

● SOURCE I

A print from a nineteenth-century 'Penny Dreadful' showing Sweeney Todd at work.

● **SOURCE J**

A photograph from the musical about Sweeney Todd which opened in London in 2003. It shows the characters of Mrs Lovett and Sweeney Todd.

Questions

1 Study **Sources A** and **B**.
How far does Source A help you decide if the story in Source B is true?
Use the sources to explain your answer. [7]

2 Study **Sources C** and **D**.
Does Source D prove that Source C is wrong?
Use the sources to explain your answer. [8]

3 Study **Sources E** and **F**.
Is one of these sources more helpful than the other in deciding if Sweeney Todd really existed?
Use the sources to explain your answer. [8]

4 Study **Source G**.
Do you believe Mrs Lovett?
Use the sources to explain your answer. [8]

5 Study **Sources H, I** and **J**.
Are you surprised that these sources give similar impressions of Sweeney Todd?
Use the sources to explain your answer. [7]

6 Study **all** the sources.
Do you think it is possible to know the truth about Sweeney Todd?
Use the sources to explain your answer. [12]

1750–1900 175
1750–1900
1750–1900
1750–1900
1750–1900
1750–1900
1750–1900
1750–1900
1750–1900
1750–1900
50–1900

The Peterloo massacre: did the authorities over-react?

Read all the sources, then answer the questions on page 49.

On 16 August 1819 a mass meeting was held on St Peter's Field, in Manchester. It was one of a series of meetings, held around the country, to demand the vote for ordinary working men. Forty minutes after this Manchester meeting officially started, it was all over. Eleven protesters were dead and hundreds of men, women and children were injured. What had gone wrong?

Local magistrates, concerned beforehand that the meeting might end in a riot, arranged for a large number of soldiers to be stationed in Manchester on that day, just in case they were needed. The 15th Hussars, regular soldiers, were stationed in two streets close by St Peter's Field. The Manchester and Salford Yeomanry Cavalry, made up of local businessmen, was there as well. All 400 of Manchester's special constables were on duty, too.

People began gathering in St Peter's Field from about 11.00a.m. The magistrates, worried by the huge numbers collecting in a relatively small space, ordered the special constables to clear a pathway between the hustings, where the speeches were to be made, and the magistrates' lodging house. By 1.20p.m. all the main speakers had arrived, including the famous orator and MP, Henry Hunt. Reporters from national and local newspapers joined the speakers on the hustings. The by now seriously alarmed magistrates decided that Manchester itself was in danger, and they ordered the local yeomanry to arrest Henry Hunt and the other speakers. The Manchester and Salford Yeomanry entered St Peter's Field along the pathway kept open by the special constables. Unused to crowd control, they laid about with their sabres in their efforts to reach the hustings. They managed to arrest the speakers, meeting organisers and newspaper reporters, but had themselves to be rescued by the 15th Hussars before they could get away. By 2.00p.m. it was all over.

Had the magistrates over-reacted to a peaceful, legal meeting?

Or had they acted properly to prevent a riot and large-scale loss of life and property?

● **SOURCE A**

On Monday afternoon a large body of no fewer than 2,000 people, started an attack. Stones were thrown and the windows smashed to atoms; the internal part of the building being guarded, a musket was fired in the hope of frightening and dispersing the attackers. In a very short time the effects were too shockingly seen in the death of three, and it is said, about ten wounded.

The *Manchester Gazette*, 2 May 1812, reporting a Luddite attack on a Manchester factory.

● **SOURCE B**

Then came the 'Blanket Meeting' in St Peter's Field, Manchester, from which thousands of men were to march to London with their petition, each carrying a blanket or rug strapped to the shoulder. Large numbers of the King's Dragoon Guards rode rapidly to the hustings, which they surrounded, and took twenty-nine Blanketeers into custody. When the field was cleared, a large body of soldiers and constables were sent after those who had already started out on the roads towards London. They found them on Lancashire Hill, near Stockport. Some hundreds were taken into custody and several received sabre wounds.

From a book called *Historical Sketches and Personal Recollections of Manchester* by Archibald Prentice. Here, he is remembering what he saw when the Blanketeers set out on 10 March 1817.

● **SOURCE C**

We are convinced that a rising against the government has been planned. So far the working people have been very calm but we do not expect this to continue. The people's feelings are stirred up by the radicals at the meetings that are being held nearly every week. We cannot prevent these meetings, so we do not know how to stop the dangerous ideas of the radicals being spread among the people.

From a report from the Manchester magistrates to Lord Sidmouth, the Home Secretary, on 1 July 1819, six weeks before the meeting on St Peter's Field.

● **SOURCE D**

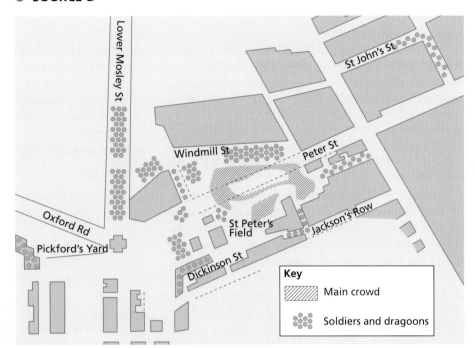

This plan of St Peter's Field, showing where the various groups of people were, was published in the *Manchester Observer* on 23 October 1819.

● **SOURCE E**

Soon after nine o'clock the people began to assemble. The majority were young persons, in their best Sunday suits, and the cheerful tidy-looking women in light coloured dresses. Slowly and orderly the multitudes took their places round the hustings, the numerous flags adding colour to the scene. I passed round the outskirts of the meeting, and mingled with the groups that stood chatting there. They laughed at the fears of the magistrates, and remarked that if the men had been intending trouble they would not have brought their wives, their sisters, or their children with them. I occasionally asked the women if they were not afraid to be there, and the usual laughing reply was 'What have we to be afraid of?'

From *Historical Sketches and Personal Recollections of Manchester* by Archibald Prentice, published in 1851. Archibald Prentice was a moderate reformer, living in Manchester, who was at St Peter's Field on 16 August 1819.

● **SOURCE F**

The Manchester Yeomanry cavalry rode into the mob which gave way before them, and directed their course to the cart from where Hunt was speaking. Not a brickbat was thrown at them – not a pistol was fired; all was quiet and orderly.

As soon as Hunt and Johnson were arrested, a cry was made by the cavalry 'Have their flags.' They immediately dashed, not only at the flags that were on the hustings, but at those that were posted among the crowd, cutting indiscriminately to the right and left in order to get at them. This set people running in all directions, and it was not until this act had been committed that any brickbats were hurled at the military. From that moment the Manchester Yeomanry Cavalry lost all command of their temper.

From a report published in *The Times* newspaper on 19 August 1819. The account was written by John Tyas, the only reporter from a national newspaper to be present at St Peter's Field on 16 August. He was on the hustings with Henry Hunt, arrested with him and imprisoned for a couple of days.

● **SOURCE G**

Mr Tyas accuses the Yeomanry of cutting, to get at the flags, after Hunt and Johnson had been taken into custody – of losing their control of temper after brickbats had been hurled at them. There is ample evidence to prove that this attack had begun before the hustings were surrounded. The temper of the Yeomanry and of all the troops employed in dispersing the crowds at the meeting, in spite of the fact that a yeoman was struck senseless from his horse, can be shown by the fact that not more than one death can be ascribed to a sabre wound.

From a letter written to *The Times* newspaper by Hugh Birley. He was complaining about the report (Source F) written by John Tyas. Hugh Birley owned a large textile factory in Manchester and was a captain in the Manchester and Salford Yeomanry Cavalry.

● **SOURCE H**

The crowd had pelted us with stones for an hour or two. Captain Booth gave the word and we then charged the crowd. My horse grew quite mad and carried me over the backs of many poor devils. I think the Reformers will not call another meeting.

From a private letter from Robert Mutrie to his friend Archibald Moore, written on 19 August 1819. Robert Mutrie was a member of the Manchester and Salford Yeomanry that arrested Henry Hunt at St Peter's Field.

● **SOURCE I**

This cartoon, called *The Peterloo Massacre*, was drawn by George Cruikshank and was published in 1819.

● SOURCE J

I had a view over the whole of St Peter's area; the number of persons assembled was estimated at 50,000; the meeting did undoubtedly strike terror into the minds of the inhabitants. Many gentlemen stated to me that they were greatly alarmed, and looking to all the circumstances, my opinion was that the town was in great danger. Manchester was a large place and contained many workshops and warehouses. The magistrates therefore decided it was necessary to issue a warrant for the arrest of the leaders. Nadin [Deputy-Constable of Manchester] refused to serve the warrant without military aid. The reason Nadin gave was perfectly satisfactory. I then wrote two letters, one to the Commander of the Manchester Yeomanry, the other to Colonel L'Estrange, the commander of the military forces in Manchester, ordering them to make the arrests.

Part of William Hulton's evidence at the trial of Henry Hunt. On 16 August 1819, William Hulton was Chairman of the Cheshire and Lancashire magistrates. He had a reputation as a man who could be relied upon to deal severely with working-class people who were expressing grievances.

● SOURCE K

The magistrates decided, at the last moment, that Hunt, and the friends who accompanied him to the hustings, should be arrested at the meeting. It was a great assemblage, and, no doubt, they thought the capture of the ringleaders in front of sixty thousand people would make them think twice about what they were doing. There was an abundance of force at hand and so resistance would have been hopeless.

From *Historical Sketches and Personal Recollections of Manchester* by Archibald Prentice, published in 1851. Archibald Prentice was a moderate reformer, living in Manchester, who was at St Peter's Field on 16 August 1819.

● SOURCE L

Was the meeting at Manchester unlawful? We believe not. Was the subject being discussed an unlawful subject? Certainly not. Was anything done at the meeting BEFORE THE CAVALRY RODE IN against the law? According to our information, the law was not broken in any way.

From an editorial in *The Times* newspaper, August 1819.

Questions

1 Study **Sources A** and **B**.
Do you agree that these sources show that Manchester in the early nineteenth century was a dangerous place?
Use the sources to explain your answer. **[5]**

2 Study **Sources A, B** and **C**.
Are you surprised that the magistrates sent this report (Source C) to Lord Sidmouth, the Home Secretary?
Use the sources and your knowledge to explain your answer. **[7]**

3 Study **Sources D** and **E**.
Does Source E prove that the reaction of the authorities shown in Source D was unnecessary?
Use the sources and your knowledge to explain your answer. **[7]**

4 Study **Sources F, G** and **H**.
All these sources were written by people who were present on St Peter's Field when the yeomanry rode in. But they all give different accounts. Which one would you trust?
Use the sources and your knowledge to explain your answer. **[8]**

5 Study **Source I**.
What is the message of this cartoon?
Use the source to explain your answer. **[6]**

6 Study **Sources J** and **K**.
Why do you think these sources disagree about the reasons for the troops being sent in to St Peter's Field on 16 August 1819?
Use the sources and your knowledge to explain your answer. **[7]**

7 Study **all** the sources.
'The magistrates completely over-reacted in the way in which they dealt with the meeting on St Peter's Field on 16 August 1819.'
How far do the sources support this view?
Use the sources and your knowledge to explain your answer. **[10]**

1750–1900 175

1750–1900

1750–1900

1750–1900

1750–1900

1750–1900

1750–1900

1750–1900

1750–1900

1750–1900

1750–1900

50–1900

SOURCE INVESTIGATION

Were Peel's Peelers respected?

Read all the sources, then answer the questions on page 53.

By the end of the eighteenth century it was clear that methods of law enforcement were out of date. They could not keep up with the increase in crime, especially in the new industrial towns. Policing was largely left to watchmen, whilst in the country each parish appointed a constable. Both were part-time and ineffective. Towards the end of the eighteenth century the first moves to set up a proper police force were made when the Bow Street Runners were set up to patrol the streets of London in the evenings and to catch thieves.

In 1829 a police force was set up for London by Sir Robert Peel. It had a uniform but the police were unarmed and wore top hats to make them look like civilians. They were nicknamed 'Peelers'. They were at first regarded with great suspicion by some and scorn by others. There was a fear that a police force controlled by central government would be a threat to everyone's liberty. Others claimed the police were a laughing stock. Pay was low and many of the first recruits were of poor quality. There was high turnover and drunkenness was a problem. Many other parts of the country were reluctant to follow London's example and only did so when forced to by the government in the 1850s. Were the new police forces successful in winning the respect of the public?

● **SOURCE A**

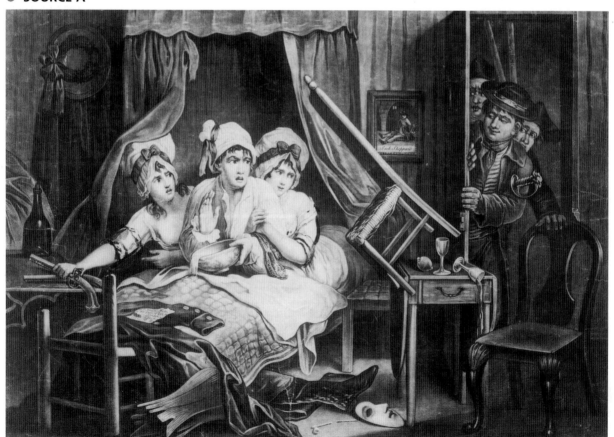

A print from 1781 showing the Bow Street Runners raiding a thieves' den.

● **SOURCE B**

A print from 1821 about watchmen.

● **SOURCE C**

It would be repulsive. It would be a plan which would make every servant of every house a spy on the actions of his master, all classes of society spies on each other.

It is difficult to have an effective system of police and that perfect freedom of action which is the great blessing of our society in this country. Your Committee think the loss of such advantages would be too great a sacrifice for improvements in the police.

From the report in 1822 of a parliamentary committee set up to look into the plans to set up a police force.

● **SOURCE D**

It should be understood that the aim is the prevention of crime. To this great end every effort of the police is to be directed. The safety of people and property will be better achieved by this than by the detection and punishment of the offender after he has succeeded in committing crime.

The constable must be careful not to interfere unnecessarily in order to make a display of his authority.

Peel's instructions to his new police force in 1829.

● **SOURCE E**

You have a very excellent uniform, and a Constable who does not take the trouble to keep it and himself clean is a discredit to the force. It is easily kept bright and clean, with its belt-plate, buttons and helmet.

Kite-flying in the streets is a very dangerous practice; and if the string breaks and the kite flaps in the face of a horse, it will frighten it; the horse may injure his rider. To put a stop to flying kites, one constable snatches the kite, snaps it in two, at which every person passing will say 'What a horrid fellow that is; the police are not at all a good sort of men.' Another constable will call out in a pleasant voice, 'My little lad go to the fields and fly your kite there', thus showing the public that whilst he has his duty to do, he has some regard for what people will think of him.

The Chief Constable of Liverpool talking to new recruits in 1852.

● **SOURCE F**

We'd 'ave lots of applicants if we paid 'alf the wages. We don't want one of these 'ere Gentlemen, who can play lawn tennis and go a-fishing, or make a nice bow in the Mayor's drawing room, or say 'ow-d'ye-do without dropping his H's. What we want is a man as can catch a thief when a chap's 'ouse is broken into.

From the memoirs of a policeman published in 1926. The policeman is remembering what was said to him when he was being interviewed for his first job in 1878.

● **SOURCE G**

Come move on there — its time you was in bed young woman any body with half an eye could see you were in liquor

A print from 1830. It shows one of Peel's policemen talking to a water pump!

● **SOURCE H**

This picture was called 'Lost in London'. It was published in a London magazine in 1888.

● **SOURCE I**

The police are beginning to take that place in the affections of the people that the soldiers and sailors used to occupy. The police – the defenders of order – are becoming the national favourites.

From a popular magazine published in 1851.

● **SOURCE J**

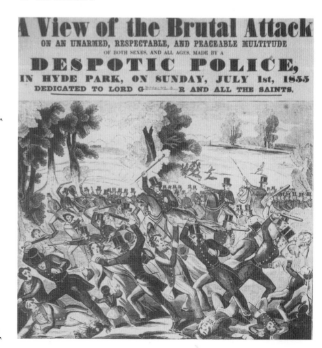

A View of the Brutal Attack
ON AN UNARMED, RESPECTABLE, AND PEACEABLE MULTITUDE
OF BOTH SEXES, AND ALL AGES, MADE BY A
DESPOTIC POLICE,
IN HYDE PARK, ON SUNDAY, JULY 1st, 1855.
DEDICATED TO LORD G⸺R AND ALL THE SAINTS.

A print from a pamphlet published in 1855.

● **SOURCE K**

WHITECHAPEL, 1888.

First Member of "Criminal Class." "FINE BODY O' MEN, THE PER-LEECE!"
Second Ditto. "UNCOMMON FINE!—IT'S LUCKY FOR HUS AS THERE'S SECH A BLOOMIN' FEW ON 'EM!!!"

A cartoon from a popular magazine, published in 1888.

Questions

1 Study **Sources A** and **B**.
According to these sources, who was more effective, the Bow Street Runners or the watchmen?
Use the sources to explain your answer. [5]

2 Study **Sources C** and **D**.
How do you think the members of the committee (Source C) would have reacted to Peel's instructions in Source D?
Use the sources and your knowledge to explain your answer. [6]

3 Study **Sources E** and **F**.
How useful are these sources as evidence about the police force in the second half of the nineteenth century?
Use the sources and your knowledge to explain your answer. [6]

4 Study **Sources G** and **H**.
Were these two pictures published for the same reason?
Use the sources and your knowledge to explain your answer. [8]

5 Study **Sources I** and **J**.
Why do you think these two sources disagree about the police?
Use the sources and your knowledge to explain your answer. [8]

6 Study **Source K**.
What is the message of this cartoon?
Use the source and your knowledge to explain your answer. [7]

7 Study **all** the sources.
Do these sources provide convincing evidence that the police were respected in the nineteenth century?
Use the sources and your knowledge to explain your answer. [10]

1750–1900
1750–1900
1750–1900
1750–1900
1750–1900
1750–1900
1750–1900
1750–1900
1750–1900
1750–1900

The Rebecca Riots

Read all the sources, then answer the questions on page 57.

In 1839 riots broke out in south-west Wales. The main target seemed to be tollgates, many of which were attacked and destroyed by groups of men, some dressed as women. Their leader was called Rebecca.

Many of the roads in this area were run by turnpike trusts who charged people for using them. Toll-gates were set up, with the gate-keeper living in the nearby toll-house. The money he collected was meant to be used for keeping the roads in good condition.

The farmers in this area made a lot of use of the roads – to take their goods to the local town to sell, and to transport lime, which they used to fertilise their land. Often different roads belonged to different trusts leading to more gates and tolls, which the farmers claimed they could not afford. Many of the farmers, and their workers, barely scraped a living from the land. Things were made worse in 1834 when payments to help the poor were stopped. The poor were forced into the hated workhouses. There were also complaints about tithes – a payment of goods such as wheat and barley that was made to the Church. In 1836 people had to pay the tithes in money, which often they did not have. Tithes were also unpopular because most of the money went to the local landowner, instead of to the vicar.

In the summer of 1843 the government sent troops into South Wales. They also set up a commission to investigate the turnpike system. A new law was passed in 1844. This allowed only one turnpike trust to operate in each county. The tolls were fixed – the trusts could not increase them, and the toll on lime was reduced by half. The riots ended in October 1843. Does this mean they had only been about the tolls?

● **SOURCE A**

An illustration of the Rebecca Rioters in 1839, published in a London newspaper at the time.

● **SOURCE B**

A print published at the time entitled 'Rebecca and her daughters assembling to destroy a Turnpike Gate'.

● **SOURCE C**

The main cause of the disturbances is the poverty of the people. The small farmer here breakfasts on oatmeal and boiled water, or on a few mashed potatoes left from the previous night's supper. He dines on potatoes and buttermilk, with sometimes a little white Welsh cheese. Fresh meat is never seen on the Farmer's table. His butter he never tastes, he sells it to pay his rent.

The condition of the farm labourers is terrible. They live entirely on potatoes, and seldom have enough of them. They have one meal a day. They live in mud cottages with only one room.

From *The Times* newspaper, 2 December 1843. *The Times* was published in London.

● **SOURCE D**

The farmers loudly complain of the oppressive nature of the tolls. They gave me an example of a road on which a gate has been erected and a sixpenny toll demanded for a horse and cart. A fortnight ago a bridge on this road was broken down by a flood. The trust refused to do anything. The farmers say there is not a road of any kind by which a cart can get to the lime-kilns which has not a gate on it. They say that if there is a road by which farmers can get to their farms without paying a toll the trusts put up gates. The trusts have surrounded the towns with gates.

From *The Times* newspaper, 4 August 1843. Written by Thomas Foster, a journalist sent by *The Times* to report. Foster had the trust of the farmers and they even chose him to be chairman when they met with the local magistrates on 8 August. At the end of the Rebecca troubles they presented him with a silver dish.

● **SOURCE E**

News soon reached Carmarthen that Rebecca and between five and six thousand of her children had gathered. Shops were closed and thousands of people had gathered along the streets to obtain a view of the procession.

A number of unruly bystanders joined them and led them along the streets. It is highly likely that those bystanders were the cause of the destruction caused by Rebecca in Carmarthen. They pushed open the doors of the workhouse. The entrance of the workhouse was now full of rioters, on foot and on horseback. Every part of the building was occupied. The men had broken into the rooms of the master, smashing the furniture and dancing on the tables.

When later the magistrates questioned some of the rioters each repeated the same story – that they had been forced to come there by the threat that their possessions be burned and they themselves killed.

From a Welsh-language newspaper, describing events on 19 June 1843 in the town of Carmarthen.

● **SOURCE F**

£500
Reward!!

Whereas on the Night of the 22nd day of August inst., a Felonious and

MURDEROUS
ATTACK

was made upon

MR. JOHN EDWARDS,

at the House of

GELLYWERNEN,

in the Parish of Llanon, in this County, by a Mob of Persons who Fired into the said House, with the Intention of taking away the Life of the said Mr. Edwards, and also did much Damage to the House at Gellywernen, and the Kitchen-Garden and Hot-houses adjoining, although Mr. Edwards providentially escaped.

A poster offering a reward for information about the attack on John Edwards in August 1843. John Edwards looked after the estate, and collected the tithes, for the local landowner. £1,000 a year was collected, but only £13 of this went to the vicar!

● **SOURCE G**

A cartoon published in a London magazine in 1841. The gatekeeper peeping round his door is Robert Peel who was Prime Minister at that time. The gateposts are members of his government.

● SOURCE H

A LETTER.

"To the Public generally, and to our Neighbours in particular.

"WE, *John Hughes, David Jones* and *John Hugh*, now lying in Cardiff gaol, convicted of the attack on Pontardulais turnpike gate, and the police stationed there to protect it–being now sentenced to transportation, beg, and earnestly call on others to take warning by our fate, and to stop in their mad course, before they fall into our condemnation.

"*We are guilty, and doomed to suffer*, while hundreds have escaped. Let them, and every one, take care not to be deluded again to attack public or private property, and resist the power of the law, for it will overtake them with vengeance, and bring them down to destruction.

Part of a letter written in November 1843 from their prison cell by three of the rioters who had been sentenced in October to be transported to Australia.

● SOURCE I

The people saw that the only answer was to take the law into their own hands. The Rebecca conspiracy was organised with much skill. It never changed from its original purpose and the minute that purpose seemed likely to be achieved, the riots were stopped and never revived.

Written by Frankland Lewis, a local magistrate, in 1852.

Questions

1 Study **Sources A** and **B**.
How far do they give similar impressions of the Rebecca Rioters?
Use the sources to explain your answer. [7]

2 Study **Sources C** and **D**.
Does Source D prove that Source C was wrong about the causes of the riots?
Use the sources and your knowledge to explain your answer. [9]

3 Study **Sources E** and **F**.
Do these two sources prove that the rioters were simply thugs?
Use the source and your knowledge to explain your answer. [7]

4 Study **Source G**.
What is the message of this cartoon?
Use the source and your knowledge to explain your answer. [7]

5 Study **Sources H** and **I**.
The riots stopped in November 1843. How far does Source I provide reliable evidence that the riots stopped because the rioters had been successful?
Use the sources and your knowledge to explain your answer. [8]

6 Study **all** the sources.
'The Rebecca Riots were caused by the actions of the turnpike trusts.'
How far do these sources support this statement?
Use the sources and your knowledge to explain your answer. [12]

SOURCE INVESTIGATION

Jack the Ripper: why was he never caught?

> **Read all the sources, then answer the questions on page 61.**

In 1888 five women were brutally murdered in the Whitechapel area of the East End of London. They were all killed within one square mile and within a three-month period, between August and November. Mary Ann Nichols, Annie Chapman, Elizabeth Stride, Catherine Eddowes and Mary Jane Kelly were all prostitutes. They all had their throats cut and their bodies mutilated. The police believed that the same man killed them all.

Prostitutes were often violently attacked, so why should these murders attract so much attention? Partly it was the gruesome nature of the murders; partly it was because the name 'Jack the Ripper' caught the attention of the media and the imagination of the public; and partly it was the hundreds of hoax letters, supposedly from 'Jack', which taunted the police for their lack of success.

The local Whitechapel police, the City of London police and detectives at Scotland Yard were all involved in tracking down the serial killer. At one point, more than 600 plain clothes officers were working on the case. But Jack the Ripper was never caught. Why not?

Known victims of Jack the Ripper
There were eleven prostitute murders in Whitechapel between April 1888 and February 1891. All have at some time been attributed to Jack the Ripper. These women are the most likely to have been his victims:

Date	Victim	Circumstances
Friday 31 August 1888	Mary Ann Nichols	Found in Buck's Row, Whitechapel. Throat cut and abdomen slashed.
Saturday 8 September 1888	Annie Chapman	Found in the back yard of 29 Hanbury Street, Spitalfields. Throat cut and disembowelled.
Sunday 30 September 1888	Elizabeth Stride	Found in Dutfield's Yard, Berner Street. Throat cut.
Sunday 30 September 1888	Catherine Eddowes	Found in Mitre Square, City of London. Throat cut, abdomen slashed open.
Friday 9 November 1888	Mary Jane Kelly	Found in Swallow Gardens, Whitechapel. Throat cut and chest cavity opened.

● **SOURCE A**

The number of Common Lodging Houses in the Whitechapel division is 233, accommodating 8,530 persons. We have no means of knowing which women are prostitutes and which are not, but there is an impression that there are about 1,200 prostitutes, mostly of a very low condition.

The worst kind of Common Lodging House is naturally frequented by prostitutes, thieves and tramps as there is nowhere else for them to go, and no law to prevent them gathering there.

Part of a confidential police report to the Home Office, 25 October 1888.

● **SOURCE B**

A photograph, taken in the 1890s, of the Sunday market in Petticoat Lane. This was in the heart of Whitechapel, the very poorest area of London, and the centre of the Jewish quarter. Most of the goods being bought and sold here were clothes, old and new.

● **SOURCE C**

Part of the front page of *The Illustrated Police News*, a popular journal that described police matters such as crimes, inquests and trials. Two of the murders shown here are those of Mary Ann Nichols and Annie Chapman, the Ripper's first two victims. The body of Mary Nichols was found in Buck's Row, Whitechapel and that of Annie Chapman in the rear yard of 29 Hanbury Street, Spitalfields.

● **SOURCE D**

He was dark and wearing a deerstalker hat. I think he was wearing a dark coat but I cannot be sure. He looked shabby, but respectable. He was a man over forty, as far as I could tell. He looked to me like a foreigner.

Part of the statement made by Elizabeth Long at the inquest into the death of Annie Chapman. She is describing the man seen talking to Annie shortly before she was killed on 8 September 1888.

● **SOURCE E**

He was aged about thirty-five and about five feet eleven inches tall. I would say he had a fresh complexion and his hair was light brown. He wore a dark overcoat, an old black hard felt hat with a wide brim. He was smoking a clay pipe.

Part of the statement made by Israel Schwartz at the inquest into the death of Elizabeth Stride. He is describing the man seen talking to Elizabeth shortly before she was killed on 30 September 1888.

● **SOURCE F**

He was aged 34–35 years old and about five feet six inches tall, with a pale complexion, dark hair and a little moustache that curled up at the ends. He wore a long dark coat with a dark jacket underneath, with dark trousers and button boots. His shirt was white and his black tie was fastened with a horseshoe shaped pin. He had a dark hat, turned down in the middle and a red kerchief. He was clearly Jewish and respectable.

Part of the statement made by George Hutchinson at the inquest into the death of Mary Kelly. He is describing the appearance of the man seen talking to her shortly before she was killed on 9 November 1888.

● **SOURCE G**

Dear Boss
I keep on hearing the police have caught me but they won't fix me just yet. I have laughed when they look so clever and talk about being on the right track. I am down on whores and shan't stop ripping them up till I do get caught. Grand job the last job was. I gave the lady no time to squeal. How can they catch me now? The next job I do I shall clip the lady's ears off and send to the police officers. My knife's so nice and sharp I want to get to work right away if I get the chance.
Yours truly
Jack the Ripper

The first letter supposedly from Jack the Ripper. It was dated 25 September 1888 and was sent to the Central News Agency in Ludgate Hill, London. The Central News Agency collected reports from correspondents throughout the world. It had a reputation for 'scoops' – getting the news ahead of other agencies.

● **SOURCE H**

The Juwes are
The men that
Will not
Be blamed
for nothing

A copy of graffiti chalked in a doorway close to where the body of Catherine Eddowes was found on 30 September 1888. Part of her bloodstained apron was found in the same doorway.

175

1750–1900

1750–1900

1750–1900

1750–1900

1750–1900

1750–1900

1750–1900

1750–1900

50–1900

● SOURCE I

The writing was on the open archway and could be seen by anybody in the street. We talked about whether it could be covered up for an hour or so until it could be photographed. But taking into consideration the strong feelings that existed in the area against the Jews, and fearing a riot, I ordered the writing to be wiped away. I took a copy of it and this I enclose.

Part of a report from Sir Charles Warren, the Chief Commissioner of the Metropolitan Police, on action taken after the body of Catherine Eddowes had been found.

● SOURCE J

The writing on the wall may have been written – and, I think, probably was written – to throw the police off the scent, to throw suspicion upon the Jews. It may have been written by the murderer, or it may not. To wipe out the words that might have given us a most valuable clue, more especially after I had sent a man to stand over them until they were photographed, was totally unreasonable.

From a book *From Constable to Commissioner* written by Major Henry Smith and published in 1910. At the time of the 'Ripper' murders, Major Henry Smith was Commissioner of the City of London Police.

Questions

1 Study **Sources A** and **B**.
What can we learn from these sources about Whitechapel at the end of the nineteenth century?
Use the sources to explain your answer. [6]

2 Study **Source C**.
People living in Whitechapel in 1888 were desperately afraid and in need of reliable information. Why would they have read this source?
Use the source and your knowledge to explain your answer. [7]

3 Study **Sources D, E** and **F**.
How far were these sources useful to the police in their search for Jack the Ripper?
Use the sources and your knowledge to explain your answer. [6]

4 Study **Source G**.
Are you surprised that this letter was written?
Use the source and your knowledge to explain your answer. [8]

5 Study **Sources H** and **I**.
'The graffiti had nothing to do with the murder and so Sir Charles Warren was quite right to rub it out.'
Use the sources and your knowledge to explain whether you agree with this statement. [7]

6 Study **Sources I** and **J**.
Was Major Henry Smith, Commissioner of the City of London Police, right to be angry with Sir Charles Warren, Chief Commissioner of the Metropolitan Police?
Use the sources and your knowledge to explain your answer. [6]

7 Study **all** the sources.
'Jack the Ripper was never caught because the police were not up to the job.'
How far do the sources support this view?
Use the sources and your knowledge to explain your answer. [10]

SOURCE INVESTIGATION

The suffragettes: why did the government treat them as criminals?

Read all the sources, then answer the questions on page 65.

In 1903, Emmeline Pankhurst and her daughters, irritated by the lack of success of the National Union of Women's Suffrage Societies (NUWSS) in obtaining votes for women, set up an alternative campaign group called the Women's Social and Political Union (WSPU). Their aim was to use more drastic methods to bring the whole issue of female suffrage to the attention of politicians and the general public. In behaving as they did, the suffragettes were acting as a pressure, or protest, group and the government could have dealt with them in many different ways. They could, for example, have talked the whole issue through and reached agreement as to the way forward. Instead, the situation became confrontational and suffragettes were treated as criminals. Why?

● **SOURCE A**

A photograph of the 'Votes for Women' rally held in Hyde Park on 21 June 1908. The rally was organised by the WSPU. It was held in response to a statement from Prime Minister Asquith that he would back a bill giving the vote to women provided it could be proved that women and the electorate wanted it.

● **SOURCE B**

We have tried every way. We have presented larger petitions than were ever presented before any other reform, we have succeeded in holding greater public meetings than men have ever held for any reform. We have faced hostile mobs at street corners. If you had the power to send us to prison, not for six months but for six years, or for the whole of our lives, the government must not think that they can stop this agitation. It will go on. We are going to win.

Comments made in court by Emmeline Pankhurst in 1908.

● **SOURCE C**

It was exactly half-past five when we alighted from the cab and threw our stones, four of them, through the window panes [of 10 Downing Street]. At intervals of fifteen minutes, relays of women who had volunteered for the demonstration, did their work. The first smashing of glass occurred in the Haymarket and Piccadilly and alarmed both pedestrians and police. A large number of women were arrested, and everybody thought that this ended the affair. But before the police had reached the station with their prisoners, the ominous crashing and splintering of plate glass began again.

Emmeline Pankhurst describes what happened one afternoon in March 1909.

● **SOURCE D**

I have no objection to revolution, if it is necessary, but I have the very strongest objection to childishness pretending to be revolution. All I can say of these window breaking expeditions is that they are simply silly and provocative. I wish the working women of the country who really care for the vote would come to London and tell these fussy middle-class damsels who are going out with their little hammers in their muffs that if they do not go home they will get their heads broken.

From a speech made by Ramsay MacDonald in 1910. He was a Labour Party MP.

● **SOURCE E**

Mrs Pankhurst led a small deputation to the very door of the House of Commons. Here stood the stout, red-faced Inspector Scantlebury, the head of the police force attached to the House, with a company of his men. He handed Mrs Pankhurst a letter from the Prime Minister – a curt refusal to see her. 'I am firmly resolved to stand here until he does see me!' she cried with blazing eyes, and threw the letter to the ground. Inspector Jarvis then began to push her away, and his policemen laid hands on the other women. To end the struggle and protect her elder companions from the violence that usually came before an arrest, Mrs Pankhurst struck the Inspector lightly on the cheek with her open hand. 'I know why you did that,' he said, but the hustling continued. 'Must I do it again?' she asked quietly. He answered 'Yes'. She struck him on the other cheek and he called to his policemen 'Take them in.'

From a book *The Suffragette Movement* written by Sylvia Pankhurst in 1931. Here she is describing an incident outside the House of Commons on 29 June 1909, involving her mother, Emmeline, and the police.

● **SOURCE F**

For hours I was beaten about the body, thrown backwards and forwards from one policeman to another. Often seized by the coat collar, dragged out of the crowd, only to be pushed helplessly into a side street while he beat one up and down one's spine until cramp seized one's legs, when he would then release one with a violent shove. Once I was thrown with my jaw against a lamp-post with such force that two of my front teeth were loosened.

From a statement made by a suffragette in November 1910. On 18 November a group of suffragettes had been protesting outside Parliament. Afterwards, 29 women complained of indecent assault by the police. The day became known as 'Black Friday'.

● **SOURCE G**

This photograph was taken by a press photographer on 'Black Friday', 18 November 1910. The policeman has knocked the woman to the ground and the man in the top hat is trying to protect her. The editor of the *Daily Mirror* put the photograph on the front page the next day. The Metropolitan Commissioner of Police tried to stop publication of the paper, but he failed.

● **SOURCE H**

It was my intention, on November 18th, to have these women removed from the scene of disorder as soon as possible and then to prosecute only those who had committed personal assaults on the police or other serious offences. The directions which I gave were not fully understood or carried out.

I believe the Metropolitan Police behaved on November 18th with the patience and humanity for which they are well known. I reject the unsupported allegations which come from that overflowing fountain of falsehood, the Women's Social and Political Union.

From Winston Churchill's evidence in March 1911 to the Committee of Enquiry about 'Black Friday'. He had been Home Secretary at the time of the event.

● **SOURCE I**

This photograph was taken in 1912. It shows Sylvia Pankhurst painting the front of the suffragettes' shop in Bow Road, London.

● **SOURCE J**

Prisoners were held down by force, flung on the floor, tied to chairs and iron bedsteads while the tube was forced up the nostrils. After each feeding the nasal pain gets worse. The wardress tried to make the prisoner open her mouth by sawing the edge of the cup along the gums, the broken edge causing cuts and severe pain. Food into the lung of one unresisting prisoner immediately caused severe choking and vomiting. She was hurriedly released next day suffering from pneumonia and pleurisy. We cannot believe that any of our colleagues will agree that this form of prison treatment is justly described in Mr McKenna's words as 'necessary medical treatment'.

From an article in the medical journal *The Lancet*, published in August 1912.

● **SOURCE K**

I have had unlimited correspondence from every section of the public who have been good enough to advise me as to what I ought to do, and among them all I have not been able to discover more than four alternative methods. The first is to let them die. That is, I should say, at the present moment, the most popular, judging by the number of letters I have received. The second is to deport them. The third is to treat them as lunatics, and the fourth is to give them the franchise. I think we should not adopt any of them.

The Home Secretary, Reginald McKenna, said this about hunger-striking in a debate in the House of Commons on 11 June 1914.

● **SOURCE L**

Those of you who can express your militancy by joining us in our anti-Government by-election policy – do so. Those of you who can break windows – break them. Those of you who can still further attack the god of property so as to make the government realise that it is as greatly endangered by Women's Suffrage as it was by the Chartists of old – do so. And my last word to the government: I cite this meeting to rebellion. You have not dared to take the leaders of Ulster for their incitement to rebellion, take me if you dare.

From a speech made by Emmeline Pankhurst, leader of the WSPU, at the Albert Hall in October 1912.

Questions

1 Study **Sources A** and **B**.
What can you learn from these sources about the suffragettes' campaign to get votes for women?
Use the sources to explain your answer. [6]

2 Study **Sources C** and **D**.
How far does Ramsay MacDonald (Source D) support the events described in Source C?
Use the sources and your knowledge to explain your answer. [7]

3 Study **Source E**.
How reliable is this source as an explanation of why Mrs Pankhurst was arrested on 29 June 1909?
Use the source and your knowledge to explain your answer. [6]

4 Study **Sources F, G** and **H**.
Do you believe what Winston Churchill (Source H) says about the treatment of the suffragettes on Black Friday, 18 November 1910?
Use the sources and your knowledge to explain your answer. [8]

5 Study **Source I**.
Are you surprised by the peaceful scene shown in this source?
Use the source and your knowledge to explain your answer. [6]

6 Study **Sources J** and **K**.
Doctors (Source J) condemned forced feeding of suffragettes on hunger strike in prison. Why, then, did the government continue with this policy?
Use the sources and your knowledge to explain your answer. [7]

7 Study **all** the sources.
'Suffragettes were criminals and the government was right to treat them as it did.'
How far do the sources support this view?
Use the sources and your knowledge to explain your answer. [10]

Conscientious objectors: what was their crime?

> **Read all the sources, then answer the questions on page 69.**

The First World War broke out in August 1914 and in Britain, as in other countries, thousands of men rushed to join the army. At first, the army relied on these enthusiastic volunteers. However, as the war dragged on, and casualties mounted, it became clear that this volunteer army wasn't going to be big enough to defeat the Germans. In 1916 the government introduced conscription, which forced all men who were between the ages of 18 and 41 to join the armed services.

The government recognised that there were some men whose consciences would not allow them to fight. Special courts, called military tribunals, were set up to decide which men could be excused military service. These tribunals consisted of army officers and respectable middle-class people like doctors and clergymen. People were excused military service if they were medically unfit, if they had jobs that were essential for the war effort, or if they could prove they had genuine reasons of conscience for not wanting to fight.

About 16,000 men refused to fight because they were conscientious objectors. Nearly all of these men would not fight on religious grounds and many of them were members of the Society of Friends (Quakers). Around 14,500 conscientious objectors worked with the armed forces as, for example, stretcher-bearers and ambulance drivers and they played as brave a part as anyone in the fight against the enemy.

This left about 1,500 men who refused to have anything at all to do with the war. They were put in prison and had their right to vote in general elections removed until five years after the war ended. But it wasn't quite as neat as this. Conscientious objectors were nicknamed 'conchies', were sneered and jeered at, called cowards and had huge problems finding jobs. Some were sent to the front, forced into military uniform and court martialled if they refused to fight; all were humiliated. Why did so many people believe that 'conchies' were criminals who deserved to be treated in this way?

● **SOURCE A**

These recruitment posters were published by the government between 1914 and 1916.

● SOURCE B

This cartoon was published in 1916 in a pacifist newspaper called *The Workers' Dreadnought*.

● SOURCE C

On my way from a No-Conscription meeting I was pushed off my bike and arrested by two policemen. At the local police station my clothes were taken from me and I slept the night on a hard board in a cell. In the morning I was taken before a magistrate and a military escort took me to a barracks. Here khaki clothes were forced on me. There were about twelve of us including my brother. We refused to drill properly. For this we were sentenced to 28 days tied spread-eagled to the wheel of a gun.

I was court martialled and sent to Newcastle prison. This old prison was a great shock, rows and rows of cells and when the door of my cell slammed on me the bottom seemed to fall out of my little world and I wondered if I would survive. I was in this cell 23 hours out of every 24. There was a tiny window high up, a hard wooden plank bed, a bucket for a toilet and dreadful food. We met other COs only in the exercise yard and we were forbidden to talk.

Len Payne, a Quaker, remembers how he was treated during the 1914–18 war.

● SOURCE D

The field court martial seemed to have an atmosphere of hostility, but I heard in a side-room as we were waiting, one officer say to another 'You know it would be monstrous to shoot these men.'

We were taken to one side of the parade ground, then led out one by one, in front of over 1,000 soldiers. I was the first of them.

An officer in charge read out my various crimes: refusing to obey a lawful command, disobedience at Boulogne, and so on, then: 'The sentence of the court is to suffer death by being shot.' There was a pause. I thought, 'Well, that's that.' Then he said 'Confirmed by the Commander-in-Chief'. 'That's double sealed it now,' I thought. Then, after a long pause: 'But commuted to penal servitude [prison] for ten years.' And that was that. What was good was that we were back in England and out of the hands of the army.

From an account given by Howard Marten, a Quaker, who was opposed to everything to do with war. He registered as a conscientious objector during the 1914–18 war and was forced to join the Non-Combatant Corps, which did jobs like driving ambulances. He was sent to France, where he refused to obey orders. He was court-martialled and, because he was in a war zone, faced execution.

● SOURCE E

It was right at the beginning that I learnt that the only people from whom I could expect sympathy were soldiers and not civilians.

I was waiting in the guardroom when five soldiers under arrest came in. When they asked me what I was in for, I was as simple as possible. 'I am a Quaker and I refused to join the army because I think that war is murder.' 'Murder?' one of them whispered, 'it's bloody murder!' As they went away they each came up to me and shook me by the hand. 'Stick to it, matey,' they said, one after the other.

From an account given by a Quaker conscientious objector.

● **SOURCE F**

Members of the Non-Combatant Corps building a military road in East Anglia. This photograph was published in the *Illustrated War News* on 23 August 1916.

● **SOURCE G**

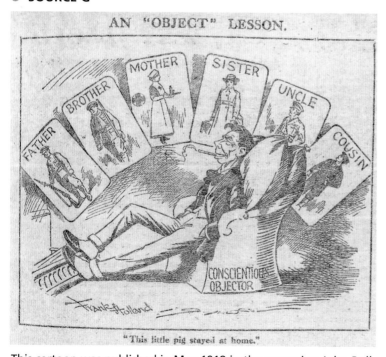

This cartoon was published in May 1918 in the magazine *John Bull*.

● **SOURCE H**

They are prepared to let other men in this country fight for their freedom, but they will not even help their country by doing any work at all for the nation.

From a speech by the government minister Lord Derby made in the House of Lords in May 1917.

● **SOURCE I**

We all recognise that there are people who have perfectly genuine and deep seated feelings on the subject of military service. Where these feelings are conscientiously held we desire that they should be respected and that there should be no persecution of those that hold them.

This was said by the Prime Minister, Neville Chamberlain, when conscription was reintroduced in 1939.

● **SOURCE J**

There was a lot of disgrace attached to being a conscientious objector. We lived for some of the war in Disley, just outside Manchester. A lot of the people in the village didn't talk to me. There was an awfully nice man there who had been terribly injured in World War One, and who was absolutely anti-war. His son was a CO and I tended to go and see people like that, just to be with people who were a bit sympathetic. Otherwise there were only two people in the village who had pacifist leanings: the lady who kept the sweet shop and the postmaster's wife. They were always nice about David, but other people took the attitude 'My son may be killed getting food for your children and what is your husband doing about it?'

The actor David Markham was sent to prison during the Second World War because he was a conscientious objector. Here, his wife Olive remembers what it was like for her.

Questions

1 Study **Source A**.
What do these posters tell you about attitudes to young men who had not volunteered to fight?
Use the source and your knowledge to explain your answer. [6]

2 Study **Source B**.
Why do you think this cartoon was published in 1916?
Use the source and your knowledge to explain your answer. [6]

3 Study **Sources C** and **D**.
Are you surprised by the ways in which these conscientious objectors were treated?
Use the sources and your knowledge to explain your answer. [7]

4 Study **Sources C**, **D** and **E**.
How far does Source E support what Len Payne and Howard Marten (Sources C and D) say about the attitudes of the military towards conscientious objectors?
Use the sources to explain your answer. [8]

5 Study **Sources F** and **G**.
'The photograph (Source F) shows conscientious objectors working on a government project, so the message of the cartoon (Source G) is wrong.'
Do you agree?
Use the sources and your knowledge to explain your answer. [6]

6 Study **Sources H**, **I** and **J**.
Would you agree that attitudes to conscientious objectors were the same in the Second World War as they had been in the First World War?
Use the sources and your knowledge to explain your answer. [7]

7 Study **all** the sources.
How far do the sources convince you that conscientious objectors deserved to be treated as criminals?
Use the sources and your knowledge to explain your answer. [10]

SOURCE INVESTIGATION

The General Strike, 1926: industrial protest or revolution?

Read all the sources, then answer the questions on page 73.

In May 1926, the country ground to a halt. For nine days, miners and transport workers, workers in the iron and steel industries, building trades, gas and electricity industries, heavy chemicals and many others stopped work. The Trades Union Congress (TUC) called them out one by one and in the end, 2.5 million workers were on strike. The TUC said they were involved in a legitimate industrial dispute. The government said it was revolution. Which side was right?

● SOURCE A

The Mining Association propose drastic reductions in the already meagre wages paid to the miners; they propose to abolish the principle of a minimum wage; to destroy the principle of national agreements and to make the national unification of the industry an impossibility.

The General Council appreciate to the full the fact that no self-respecting body of organised workers could negotiate on such terms.

The General Council particularly approve of the steadfast opposition of the Miners' Federation to any proposals for a lengthened working day.

The General Council are confident they will have the backing of the whole organised Trade Union Movement in placing themselves unreservedly at the disposal of the Miners' Federation to assist the Federation in any way possible.

From a statement made to the press from the General Council of the TUC on 11 July 1925.

● SOURCE B

A general strike is not an industrial dispute; it is a revolutionary movement, intended to inflict suffering upon the great mass of innocent persons in the community and thus to force its will upon the government.

It is a movement that can only succeed by destroying government and undermining the rights and liberties of the people. This being the case, it cannot be tolerated by any civilised government and it must be dealt with by every resource at the disposal of the community. A state of emergency and national danger has been proclaimed to resist attack.

Part of the editorial in the *Daily Mail* newspaper on 3 May 1926. This was the edition union members refused to print.

● **SOURCE C**

THE
BRITISH WORKER
OFFICIAL STRIKE NEWS BULLETIN
Published by The General Council of the Trades Union Congress

No. 1.   WEDNESDAY EVENING, MAY 5, 1926.   PRICE ONE PENNY

IN LONDON AND THE SOUTH	**WONDERFUL RESPONSE TO THE CALL**	**SOUTH WALES IS SOLID!**
Splendid Loyalty of Transport Workers	General Council's Message: Stand Firm and Keep Order	Not a Wheel Turning in Allied Industries
EVERY DOCKER OUT		**'MEN ARE SPLENDID!'**

Part of the front page of the first edition of *The British Worker*, published on 5 May 1926. This was published by the Trades Union Congress.

● **SOURCE D**

The British Gazette
Published by His Majesty's Stationery Office.

No. 1.   LONDON, WEDNESDAY, MAY 5, 1926.   ONE PENNY.

FIRST DAY OF GREAT STRIKE

Not So Complete as Hoped by its Promoters

PREMIER'S AUDIENCE OF THE KING

Miners and the General Council Meet at House of Commons

FOOD SUPPLIES

No Hoarding: A Fair Share for Everybody

HOLD-UP OF THE NATION

Government and the Challenge

NO FLINCHING

The Constitution or a Soviet

COMMUNIST LEADER ARRESTED

Mr. Saklatvala, M.P., Charged at Bow Street

SEQUEL TO MAY DAY SPEECH

THE "BRITISH GAZETTE" AND ITS OBJECTS

Reply to Strike Makers' Plan to Paralyse Public Opinion

REAL MEANING OF THE STRIKE

Conflict Between Trade Union Leaders and Parliament

Part of the front page of the first edition of *The British Gazette*, published on 5 May 1926. This was published by the government.

● **SOURCE E**

Up came lorries with barbed wire all round their canopies and troops with guns sitting behind the barbed wire. The people were jeering and booing but that was the extent of their reactions. It was quite good humoured.

Then the police started pushing and pushing us into the road. This led to arguments. Before we knew it, the police were hitting us with their truncheons. There were quite a few broken arms because of police violence.

The next day the strikers were prepared for trouble. They armed themselves with iron railings ripped out of garden walls. Again the lorries with troops to guard them came up and again the police lined up, some in front but most at the back of the onlookers. Again the pushing began but this time before the police could start anything, the crowd turned on them and started laying about them with the iron railings. That day it was the police who were injured.

An account of what happened in Victoria Dock Road, London by Harry Watson, an eyewitness. This account was published in 1976 in a book about the General Strike.

● SOURCE F

The General Council of the Trades Union Congress wishes to emphasise the fact that this is an industrial dispute. The outbreak of any disturbance would be very damaging to the prospects of a successful ending of the dispute. The Council asks pickets especially to avoid obstruction and to confine themselves strictly to their legitimate duties.

Part of a message issued to all workers by the Trades Union Congress. It was printed in *The British Worker*.

● SOURCE G

UNDER WHICH FLAG?

JOHN BULL. ' ONE OF THESE TWO FLAGS HAS GOT TO COME DOWN—AND IT WON'T BE MINE."

This cartoon was published in the magazine *Punch* in May 1926.

● SOURCE H

THE LEVER BREAKS.

This cartoon was published in the magazine *Punch* in May 1926.

● SOURCE I

The Carstairs strike committee took the view that there was no point in making enemies of the police. 'If they left us alone, we would leave them alone.' The police were just as anxious to avoid trouble. The Chief Constable explained that they 'didn't want to use batons or anything like that' and suggested a football match. This sort of thing happens in the country. You get to know the policemen and they know you. The match went ahead and the strike committee scored three goals against the police.

Bill Ballantyne remembers the attitudes of the police and strike committee in Carstairs, a small town in rural Scotland, south-east of Glasgow.

● **SOURCE J**

This photograph shows mounted police getting ready to make a baton charge against a group of strikers in Walworth, south London, in May 1926.

Questions

1 Study **Source A**.
Does this source explain why there was a general strike in May 1926?
Use the source and your knowledge to explain your answer. [6]

2 Study **Source B**.
Are you surprised that union members refused to print this edition of the *Daily Mail*?
Use the source and your knowledge to explain your answer. [7]

3 Study **Sources C** and **D**.
These sources give different views about the first day of the General Strike. Which one do you trust to be telling the truth?
Use the sources and your knowledge to explain your answer. [7]

4 Study **Sources E** and **F**.
'These sources show that the TUC had lost control of the situation.' Do you agree?
Use the sources and your knowledge to explain your answer. [6]

5 Study **Sources G** and **H**.
Both these cartoons were published in the magazine *Punch* in May 1926.
Is the message of the cartoons the same?
Use the sources and your own knowledge to explain your answer. [7]

6 Study **Sources I** and **J**.
'The photograph (Source J) proves that the police were not in sympathy with the strikers.'
How far do you agree with this statement?
Use the sources and your knowledge to explain your answer. [7]

7 Study **all** the sources.
'Britain was clearly facing a revolution in 1926.'
How far do the sources convince you that this statement is correct?
Use the sources and your knowledge to explain your answer. [10]

Prisons across time

During Roman times and the Middle Ages there were few prisons. They were usually used only for prisoners who were waiting for trial or execution.

By the eighteenth century the prison system was a mess. There were more than 300 prisons in England. Many were very small and under private ownership, others were run by local authorities. The main feature of most of them was complete disorder. Jailers were paid by charging prisoners fees, selling them beer or charging visitors fees. Some of the large London prisons were full of debtors who brought their wives and children with them. In 1776 Fleet Prison contained 242 debtors and 475 wives and children. No attempt was made to regulate the prisoner's day. Friends brought them food and freely mixed with the prisoners. Indeed, it was often difficult to tell who was a prisoner and who was a visitor! Many prisoners carried on their businesses while in prison. Others passed their time gambling and getting drunk.

Under the Bloody Code most convicted people were transported, executed or put in a pillory or whipped. However by the 1830s transportation and the death penalty were being used less and prisons became much more important. For some time there had been a debate about the purpose of prison. Was it to punish, to deter, or to reform? This debate led to a different kind of prison emerging – quiet and orderly with prisoners in uniforms and masks. Prisoners were confined to identical cells and their lives were carefully regulated. But did these changes mean that prisons had improved?

Read all the sources, then answer the questions on page 77.

● **SOURCE A**

The prison was a deep underground dungeon, no larger than a dining room that could hold nine people. It was dark and noisy because of the large numbers of people there all waiting to be executed. With so many shut up in such close quarters, the poor wretches were reduced to the appearance of brutes. The stench was so terrible it could scarcely be endured.

An eyewitness description of a Roman prison in the first century BC.

● **SOURCE B**

A drawing of a sixteenth-century prison.

SOURCE C

The prison is a room, or passage, 23 feet by 7, with only one small window, and three dungeons, or cages, on the side opposite these are about 6 feet deep and about 8 feet long. One of these is for women. They are all very offensive; no chimney; no water; no sewers; damp earth floors; no infirmary. The court is not secure and the prisoners are seldom permitted to go out to it. Indeed the whole prison is out of repair. I once found the prisoners chained two or three together. Their food was put down to them through a hole in the floor of the room above; and those who served them there, often caught the fatal fever. At my first visit, I found the keeper, his assistant, and all the prisoners but one, sick of it; and heard that a few years before many prisoners had died of it – and the keeper and his wife in one night.

A description of the prison in Launceston, Cornwall, from John Howard's *State of Prisons*, published in 1777. Between 1774 and 1786 Howard travelled 50,000 miles visiting prisons in England and Europe.

SOURCE E

A PEEP into ILCHESTER BASTILE

The front page of a pamphlet about Ilchester Prison, published in 1821. The pamphlet claimed prisoners were being abused. 'Bastile' was the name of the eighteenth-century prison in Paris, which had a dreadful reputation.

SOURCE D

A print of Fleet Prison, published in 1809.

● **SOURCE F**

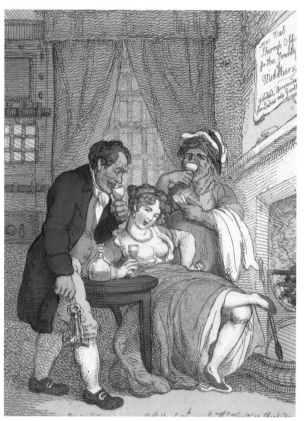

A print published in 1811 showing Kitty Careless, a prostitute, in jail.

● **SOURCE G**

A drawing of a prisoner's cell around 1850.

● **SOURCE H**

A drawing of a prisoner's cell in 1860. The prisoner is operating a crank.

● **SOURCE I**

CONVICTS EXERCISING IN PENTONVILLE PRISON.

A drawing of prisoners in 1862 in the exercise yard at Pentonville Prison.

● **SOURCE J**

Women prisoners in Brixton Prison in 1862.

● **SOURCE K**

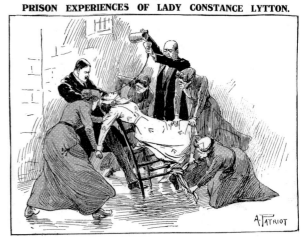

A poster from 1913 showing a woman prisoner being force-fed.

Questions

1 Study **Sources A** and **B**.
Do these sources show that prisons had changed little between Roman times and the sixteenth century?
Use the sources and your knowledge to explain your answer. [6]

2 Study **Sources C** and **D**.
In what ways are these two sources useful as evidence about prisons at this time?
Use the sources and your knowledge to explain your answer. [6]

3 Study **Sources E** and **F**.
How reliable do you think these two sources are?
Use the sources and your knowledge to explain your answer. [8]

4 Study **Sources G** and **H**.
Why did they keep prisoners in cells like these in the middle of the nineteenth century?
Use the sources and your knowledge to explain your answer. [6]

5 Study **Source I**.
How different is the treatment of these prisoners from that shown in Sources G and H?
Use the sources and your knowledge to explain your answer. [7]

6 Study **Sources J** and **K**.
Do these two sources show that the treatment of women in prisons was getting worse?
Use the sources and your knowledge to explain your answer. [7]

7 Study **all** the sources.
How far do these sources show that prisons improved over time?
Use the sources and your knowledge to explain your answer. [10]

Revision charts

Chronology

Chronology means getting events in the right order. You need to know, for example, that the Romans came before the Middle Ages and were a long time before people like Robert Peel and Elizabeth Fry in the nineteenth century. The timeline below will help you get all this sorted out. Don't worry too much about exact dates, but do worry about getting the main periods in the right order and knowing roughly how far apart different periods were from each other, for example, which is the bigger gap – between the Romans and the nineteenth century, or between the nineteenth century and today?

Important people

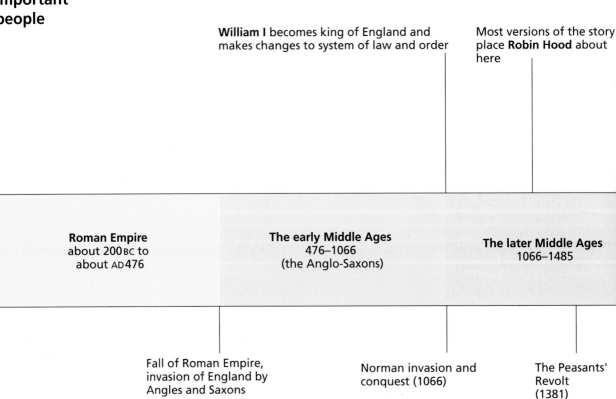

William I becomes king of England and makes changes to system of law and order

Most versions of the story place **Robin Hood** about here

Roman Empire
about 200 BC to about AD 476

The early Middle Ages
476–1066
(the Anglo-Saxons)

The later Middle Ages
1066–1485

Fall of Roman Empire, invasion of England by Angles and Saxons

Norman invasion and conquest (1066)

The Peasants' Revolt (1381)

Important events

When we are studying the history of crime and punishment we divide up the past into the periods shown below. The most important individuals in the history of crime and punishment have been added so you can see the whole picture. You need to be able to match each important individual with the right period. You also need to be able to say what each person did.

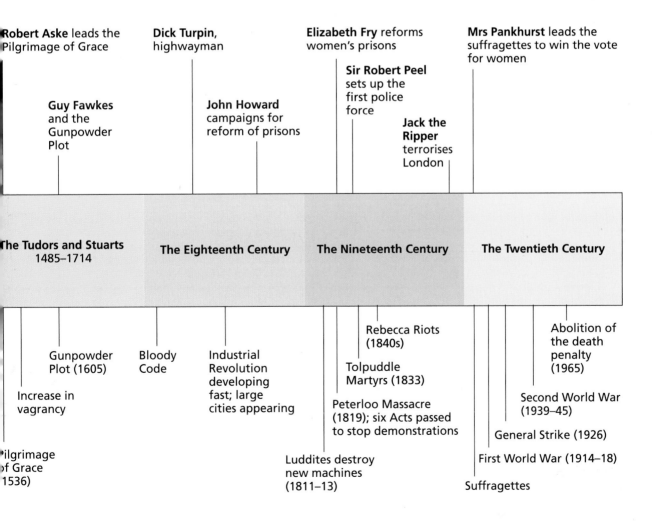

Robert Aske leads the Pilgrimage of Grace

Dick Turpin, highwayman

Elizabeth Fry reforms women's prisons

Mrs Pankhurst leads the suffragettes to win the vote for women

Guy Fawkes and the Gunpowder Plot

John Howard campaigns for reform of prisons

Sir Robert Peel sets up the first police force

Jack the Ripper terrorises London

The Tudors and Stuarts 1485–1714

The Eighteenth Century

The Nineteenth Century

The Twentieth Century

Increase in vagrancy

Gunpowder Plot (1605)

Bloody Code

Industrial Revolution developing fast; large cities appearing

Rebecca Riots (1840s)

Tolpuddle Martyrs (1833)

Peterloo Massacre (1819); six Acts passed to stop demonstrations

Abolition of the death penalty (1965)

Second World War (1939–45)

General Strike (1926)

Pilgrimage of Grace (1536)

Luddites destroy new machines (1811–13)

First World War (1914–18)

Suffragettes

Different types of crime

People in the past have had many different ideas about what is and is not a crime.

- Some things have nearly always been regarded as crimes and seem to have been around in all periods in the past – for example, stealing and murder. However, as you can see, different things have been stolen at different times in the past.
- Other things, such as having certain religious beliefs, demonstrating, or being a witch, have only been crimes at certain times when society in general or the government disapproved of them.

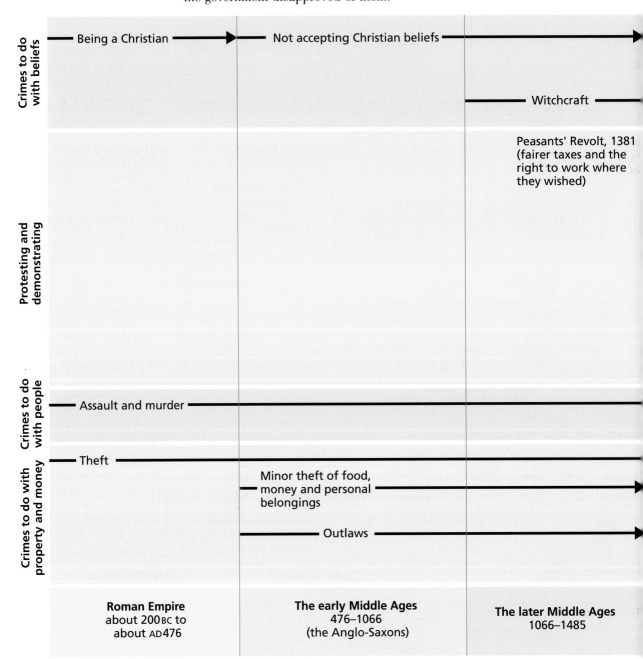

Crimes to do with beliefs	Being a Christian	Not accepting Christian beliefs	
			Witchcraft
Protesting and demonstrating			Peasants' Revolt, 1381 (fairer taxes and the right to work where they wished)
Crimes to do with people	Assault and murder		
Crimes to do with property and money	Theft	Minor theft of food, money and personal belongings	
		Outlaws	
	Roman Empire about 200 BC to about AD 476	**The early Middle Ages** 476–1066 (the Anglo-Saxons)	**The later Middle Ages** 1066–1485

- Some crimes have become very common at certain times, but less so in other periods – for example, smuggling and poaching.
- Some crimes have appeared because of new inventions – for example, car crime, computer crime.
- Some people would argue that some people were driven to crimes such as stealing food because of events – for example, stealing at times of poor harvests and high bread prices.
- Sometimes there were disagreements at the time over whether something was really a crime – for example, smuggling and poaching in the eighteenth century.

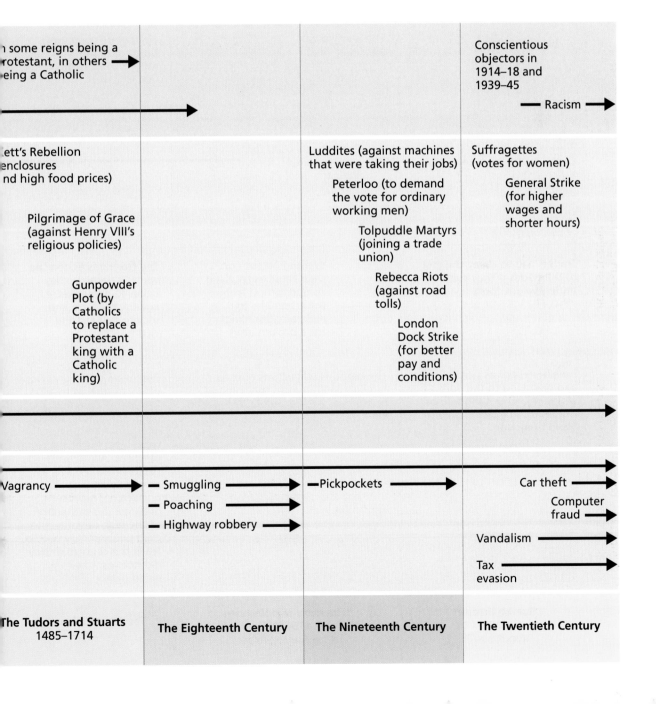

| The Tudors and Stuarts 1485–1714 | The Eighteenth Century | The Nineteenth Century | The Twentieth Century |

Punishments through the ages

Many different types of punishments have been used. The main reason for this has been different ideas about the purpose of punishment. Here are some of the main ideas. Match these ideas to each of the punishments shown on the timeline. Remember, more than one idea might relate to some of the punishments.

- To deter – to make the punishment so dreadful that it stops people from committing crimes out of fear.
- To humiliate the criminal – this is very similar to the one above – a deterrent.

	Roman Empire about 200 BC to about AD 476	**The early Middle Ages** 476–1066 (the Anglo-Saxons)	**The later Middle Ages** 1066–1485
Fines		The wergild was a form of fine.	Fines were commonly used for minor offences, especially in local manor courts.
Imprisonment	Prisons only used for people awaiting trial or execution.	Prisons only used for people waiting for their trial.	
Compensation	Traders had to repay the cost of the goods if they sold under-weight food.	Wergild (victims or their families received compensation from the criminal – for example, 6 shillings for a broken arm).	The Normans ended the wergild because they believed crimes were against the king and society, not just the victim.
Physical	Execution such as crucifixion and being fed to the lions, whipping, amputating limbs. Nobles could go into exile to avoid execution.	The blood-feud (victims or their families could punish the criminal themselves – for example, they could kill a murderer).	Execution used for serious offences such as treason. Mutilation commonly used. The pillory, stocks and public whipping were used for minor offences. An accused person who refused to attend court was outlawed. This meant they lost the protection of the law. Anyone who claimed sanctuary had to leave the country if they did not want to stand trial.

- To compensate the victim – this approach regards crime as something between the criminal and the victim, and not an act against society in general.
- To protect society in general – this approach regards crime as being against everyone in a society. It also sees punishment as a way of protecting everyone by making sure the criminal cannot commit any more crimes.
- To make the criminal suffer – this approach takes the view that the criminal has done something wrong and should be made to suffer because of it.
- To reform the criminal – this approach thinks it is important that when the criminal is released he or she will not commit any more crimes and will become a useful member of society.

The Tudors and Stuarts 1485–1714	The Eighteenth Century	The Nineteenth Century	The Twentieth Century
Catholics were fined. There were fines for not attending church and for swearing and gambling.			Fines commonly used for motoring offences and many minor offences.
	Prisons used for debtors and increasingly used for many other offences. Prisons becoming overcrowded and hulks started to be used.	Prison sentences are the most common form of punishment. Prisons made more orderly – the 'silent policy' and the 'separate policy' and the aim to reform prisoners.	Borstals set up for juvenile offenders. Probation introduced.
			Community Service Orders introduced.
Hanging, drawing and quartering. Vagrants were carted, whipped and branded. Heretics were burned at the stake.	Transportation to America. The Bloody Code introduced the death penalty for many minor offences. Transportation to Australia.	Executions only used for murder and treason. Transportation ended. Public executions ended.	Capital punishment abolished

— Public executions → very popular.

Preventing crime, catching and trying criminals

Many societies have learned that it is no good having harsh punishments if criminals are not caught. Methods of catching criminals have changed from period to period. The biggest change has been moving responsibility for this

	Roman Empire about 200 BC to about AD 476	The early Middle Ages 476–1066 (the Anglo-Saxons)	The later Middle Ages 1066–1485
Deciding if someone is guilty	Trials consisted of the suspect and the victim giving evidence and a jury deciding.	Manorial courts were held by landowners for minor offences. Trial by compurgation (juries used their knowledge of the accused and the complainant to say which one was telling the truth). Trial by ordeal – for example, hot iron, hot water, consecrated bread or cold water.	Normans introduced trial by battle. Church courts were set up to try sexual and moral cases. Their aim was to reform not to punish. Sheriffs and JPs were appointed to try people in local courts. Royal judges visited every area regularly to hear serious cases. Juries were used to hear evidence and decide if the accused was innocent or guilty.
Catching criminals	People who were attacked or robbed had to catch the criminal themselves.	The hue and cry – victims had to catch the criminals themselves. They could call out local people to help them. Men were grouped into tens called tithings. If one of them broke the law the others had to bring him to court.	Sheriffs were appointed to track down criminals and take them to court. Juries of presentment had to give sheriffs names of those suspected of crimes.
Preventing crime	*Vigiles* were used to stop crime and put out fires. Urban cohorts (soldiers) were used to prevent riots.	Village constables were appointed (unpaid and part-time) to keep order. The king's army was used to deal with major uprisings.	→

from individuals and local communities to official bodies such the government and police forces. More recently, some people have argued that preventing crime is as important as catching criminals after crimes have been committed.

Once someone has been arrested there is the difficult task of deciding if they are guilty or not. There have been many different methods used to do this.

The Tudors and Stuarts 1485–1714	The Eighteenth Century	The Nineteenth Century	The Twentieth Century
'Swimming' and evidence of the Devil's marks on women's bodies were used as evidence of witchcraft.	Prosecution and defence lawyers begin to be used in courts.		
Witchfinders such as Matthew Hopkins.		Bow Street Runners were set up in London to catch thieves. Sir Robert Peel set up the first police force in London. It became compulsory for all towns and counties to set up police forces. First detective force was set up in London.	First women police officers were appointed. Specialist squads such as the Anti-Terrorist Squad and the Fraud Squad were set up.
Night watchmen were appointed in London and other towns to patrol the streets and keep order.		Bow Street Runners were set up in London to patrol the streets in the evenings. Sir Robert Peel set up the first police force in London. At first, its most important job was to prevent crime.	

Factors

Crime and punishment has sometimes been influenced by factors such as government, religion or the work of individuals. There are often questions in the examination about these factors. Some examples are given later to help you prepare for these types of questions. Remember – these factors sometimes work together with other factors; as you can see from the example of the setting up of the Metropolitan Police Force in 1829. Try to find other examples.

Industrialisation
The Industrial Revolution led to the rapid growth of towns in the eighteenth and nineteenth centuries. Hundreds of thousands of people were crammed into these towns. This led to an increase in crime, with which constables and watchmen were completely unable to cope. A new system was needed.

The role of government
At this time it was slowly becoming accepted that government should be more involved in many areas of people's lives. It was also becoming accepted that governments should levy taxes to pay for these new activities. The setting up of the police force is just one example of increased government activity at this time.

Individuals
Sir Robert Peel was the member of the government in charge of law and order. He realised that the old systems were inadequate. He experimented first with Bow Street patrols. Twenty-seven men patrolled by day, looking out for suspicious activities. Peel developed this into the Metropolitan Police Force in 1829.

exam tip ▶ *Use specific examples, don't waffle*

Do not give general answers such as 'The development of large cities led to more problems in crime and punishment.' Use a specific example, such as how and why the problems caused by industrialisation led to the police force being set up. When you go into the exam room make sure you know two or three examples of each factor that affects crime and punishment. When you write your answer make sure you use these examples.

exam tip ▶ *Don't just describe an example of a factor*

For example, you must not simply describe the new industrial cities – you must explain why the conditions in these cities made a police force necessary and how this helped Peel discover a new approach.

exam tip ▶ *Make sure you read the question carefully*

If the question asks for reasons why the first police force was set up in 1829 don't explain just one reason – make sure you explain how there were two or three reasons. Try to show how these reasons acted together to bring about the change. However, if the question asks you to explain how government has had an influence on crime and punishment, you need to explain several separate examples such as the setting up of the police, the government introducing the Bloody Code in the eighteenth century, and the government changing prisons in the nineteenth century.

Government

The role of government is one of the most important factors in crime and punishment because governments have the power to change things. For much of the past it has been the job of the government to maintain law and order.

- Governments make the laws and it is these that turn certain activities and beliefs into crimes.
- Governments also decide what kinds of trial and what punishments will be used.
- Today governments are responsible for catching criminals, but this was not always the case.
- Sometimes governments' actions have had consequences on crime and punishments that were unintended.
- Remember that sometimes changes were caused by a number of different reasons, not just government. Sometimes other factors such as religion were present. Sometimes governments were reacting to what people at the time wanted; at other times they were protecting the interests of a small group, such as landowners.

Find one example from the following list of each of the categories mentioned above. After reading through the list, decide if you agree with this statement: governments have gradually got more and more involved in crime and punishment.

1 Although the Roman government didn't do much in terms of catching criminals, it did pass laws. An example is when the Roman Emperor decided that Christianity would be the religion of the empire. This meant it was no longer a crime to be a Christian. You can see that whether someone was a criminal or not depended on what the law said. A Christian was a criminal one moment, but not the next!

2 In Roman times if someone committed a crime against you, it was your job to catch the criminal and collect the evidence against that person. The government provided the judge and the court for the trial but that was all.

3 In Anglo-Saxon times things were not very different. Villagers had to catch criminals by raising the hue and cry, and they were expected to give up a member of their tithing to the court if they broke the law. Even manorial courts were run by the local landowner and not by the government.

4 The Normans kept many of the Saxon laws but they also made changes. They introduced the forest laws that made it illegal in certain areas to cut down trees for fuel and building. People in forests could not own dogs or arrows.

5 The Normans introduced trial by battle and ordered that fines should be paid to the king's officials instead of to the victim as compensation. This was because the king's peace had been broken.

6 The Normans thought that if someone broke the law this was not just a matter between the criminal and the victim. They thought that the king's peace had been broken – so it was a matter for the government. Royal courts were set up all over the country to try criminals, and royal judges travelled the country to hear these cases.

If people break the law they are breaking my law so I will punish them and I will collect the fines.

7 The Normans used the sheriff to track down and imprison criminals. However, the local community still helped. They provided the posse that helped the sheriff. Part-time constables and watchmen from the local community also helped to keep law and order. The role of the government was increasing but the local community still did a lot of the work.

8 In the sixteenth century governments were worried about the number of vagrants. Harsh punishments were introduced such as branding, slavery, whipping and even execution. However, people who were poor and unemployed through no fault of their own received help.

9 In the sixteenth century witchcraft was made a crime. In the eighteenth century a law was passed that meant it was no longer a crime!

10 In the sixteenth century some monarchs were Protestant and others were Catholic. In one reign it was illegal to be a Catholic, in the next reign it was the other way round!

11 In the seventeenth and eighteenth centuries governments increased taxes on imported goods. This led to a massive increase in smuggling.

12 In the eighteenth century it was the government that introduced the Bloody Code. It thought the best way to stop people committing crimes was to make punishments as harsh as possible. Even minor crimes were punished by execution. Many ordinary people believed that activities such as poaching and smuggling were not crimes – but the government disagreed. Many landowners supported the government in what they were doing.

I have to go poaching and smuggling otherwise my family will starve. The government is just looking after the landowners.

13 In the eighteenth century the government introduced the new punishment of transportation.

14 In the early nineteenth century the government abolished the Bloody Code because it was unpopular and was not working. Prison was used a lot more.

15 In the nineteenth century the government introduced the silent and separate systems into prisons. Influenced by individuals such as John Howard and Elizabeth Fry, the government started to try to reform prisoners.

16 In 1829 Sir Robert Peel and the government set up the Metropolitan Police Force. In 1856 the government made it compulsory for all towns and counties to set up police forces. This shows clearly that the government now thought the prevention of crime and the catching of criminals was its responsibility.

The crime rate in many large cities is so high that the government will have to set up police forces.

17 As governments became more involved in every aspect of society, new laws were passed creating new offences. For example, it became an offence to fail to send your children to school, and in the twentieth century sexual and racial discrimination, car and computer offences became crimes. At the same time laws were passed giving people more freedom such as the freedom to join trade unions, to hold religious beliefs of their choice and to demonstrate. You can see that government actions were influenced by a number of factors such as new inventions and new attitudes in society.

18 In 1965 the government abolished capital punishment despite the majority of people wanting to keep it.

Religion

Religious beliefs obviously influence what people think is right and wrong. So they are likely to have had an effect on what people have regarded as crimes and how they thought criminals should be punished.

- Remember that in many periods in the past religion was very important to most people. It governed how they lived many aspects of their lives. People also believed it was right to force their religious beliefs on others because in the long run it would help them get to heaven. This led to terrible persecution and punishments being used for religious reasons.
- At other times religion has led people to fight for less harsh punishments and for better conditions in prisons.
- As you have already seen religion has also had an important effect on how governments have acted towards crime and punishment.
- There have been times when the Church has challenged the government over who had the right to try and punish certain people.
- Religion has sometimes led to people rebelling, plotting or protesting against the government.

1 There have been many times in the past when governments have made certain religious beliefs illegal and have persecuted people who followed these beliefs. You can find examples of this in the list about government (pages 87–88).

2 Governments have used terrible punishments for those who have held the wrong religious beliefs. People were fed to the lions by the Romans and burned at the stake in the sixteenth century by monarchs such as Henry VIII and Mary I. Because religion was powerful it often led to the worst punishments such as hanging, drawing and quartering. Monarchs thought that someone acting against the official religion was a threat to the government and so was guilty of treason.

3 The Saxons and people later in the Middle Ages used trial by ordeal. This was based on religious beliefs. An ordeal (by hot iron, hot or cold water, or consecrated bread) was used when a jury could not reach a decision. God was then asked to decide. Before the ordeal, the accused had to fast and go to church. The ordeal often took place in a church.

4 The Normans introduced trial by battle. The accused and the alleged victim fought. The loser, if not killed, was then hanged. People believed that God could give his judgement in this way. God would not allow an innocent man to be defeated in battle.

Come on God, give us a helping hand!

5 In the Middle Ages and through to the seventeenth century, church courts operated alongside the king's courts. Many of the offences they dealt with were sexual. They also dealt with offences that could be described as immoral behaviour, such as failure to attend church, drunkenness and wife-beating. The role of the church courts was to reform rather than just punish people. Most offenders had to do public penance.

6 In the Middle Ages the practice of 'benefit of clergy' developed because the Church claimed that only its courts should deal with the clergy. Clergy included not just priests and bishops but anyone who could read a passage from the Bible! Church courts could not impose the death penalty – anyone accused of a serious crime would much rather go to a church court where instead of being executed you were branded on the thumb with a M (murderer) or a T (thief). Even in the eighteenth century thousands of people were escaping the death penalty by this method.

7 In the Middle Ages it was possible for a criminal on the run to seek sanctuary in a church, where he was protected for 40 days. He then had to decide to agree to be tried or to be exiled from the country.

8 Religious beliefs were partly behind rebellions such as the Pilgrimage of Grace and acts like the Gunpowder Plot.

9 In the sixteenth and seventeenth centuries religious divisions between Catholics and Protestants, and religious beliefs about the Devil, had a lot to do with fears over witches. The Church's teaching that women were more likely than men to be won over by the Devil was also a factor.

10 In the eighteenth century the bodies of hanged criminals were sometimes dissected. To have your body dissected was part of the sentence handed down by the judge and was meant to be a deterrent to criminals. This was because people believed that their bodies could not be resurrected at the Day of Judgement if they had been dissected.

11 In the eighteenth and nineteenth centuries religious beliefs led reformers such as John Howard and Elizabeth Fry to campaign for better conditions in prisons. The terrible conditions they both found in prisons went directly against their belief in Christian charity. They wanted prisoners to be treated with humanity and to be helped to lead Christian lives in the future. Fry taught women prisoners to read from the Bible.

These church courts are becoming a nuisance. They are letting criminals off lightly.

12 In the First and Second World Wars religious beliefs led some people to become conscientious objectors. They refused to join the armed forces because they thought it was wrong to kill other human beings. During the First World War most of them were sent to prison and suffered solitary confinement and hard labour.

13 When the death penalty was abolished in 1965 one of the arguments against its use was that it was unchristian to take the life of another human being. However, other Christians have used passages from the Bible to defend the use of the death penalty.

exam tip When you go into the exam room make sure you know two or three examples of how government and religion have affected crime and punishment. Be ready to explain these examples.

Other factors

Many other factors have had an influence on crime and punishment:

- Individuals
- Industrialisation and the growth of large towns
- War
- Self-interest

Remember that each of these usually acted in combination with other factors. The following examples show different factors combining. Can you work out what they are in each example?

1 John Howard and Elizabeth Fry were influenced by their religious beliefs when they tried to improve conditions in prisons

2 During the First World War newspapers were censored and people were banned from flying kites and giving bread to dogs! In both the First and Second World Wars the government introduced conscription, which led to conscientious objectors. Most of them were punished.

3 In the eighteenth century the government was full of landowners (they were the only people who could vote). This was one of the reasons for the Bloody Code being introduced. The death penalty was introduced for offences such as poaching, stealing and damaging trees in order to protect the property of landowners.

exam tip For the big changes in crime and punishment – for example, the changes introduced by the Normans, the introduction of transportation or the reform of prisons – there were several different reasons. Make sure you can explain how these different reasons combined to bring the changes about.

Index